SECOND EDITION

HUMANITY, DIVERSITY, & THE LIBERAL ARTS

THE FOUNDATION OF A COLLEGE EDUCATION

JOSEPH B. CUSEO
AARON THOMPSON

Kendall Hunt
publishing company

Book Team
Chairman and Chief Executive Officer Mark C. Falb
President and Chief Operating Officer Chad M. Chandlee
Vice President, Higher Education David L. Tart
Director of National Book Program Paul B. Carty
Product/Development Supervisor Lynne Rogers
Vice President, Operations Timothy J. Beitzel
Project Coordinator Charmayne McMurray
Permissions Editor Caroline Kieler
Cover Designer Heather Richman

Cover image Shutterstock.com

Copyright © 2010, 2015 by Kendall Hunt Publishing Company

ISBN 978-1-4652-6526-5

All rights reserved. No part of this publication may be reproduced, stored in a retrieval system, or transmitted, in any form or by any means, electronic, mechanical, photocopying, recording, or otherwise, without the prior written permission of the copyright owner.

Printed in the United States of America

Brief Contents

CHAPTER 1 Liberal Arts: The Meaning and Purpose of General Education   1

CHAPTER 2 Benefits of the Liberal Arts   37

CHAPTER 3 The Meaning and Purpose of Diversity   67

CHAPTER 4 The Relationship between Liberal Arts and Diversity   101

CHAPTER 5 Tying It All Together: Developing a Plan for Making the Most of the Liberal Arts and Diversity   131

APPENDIX   171

REFERENCES   187

Contents

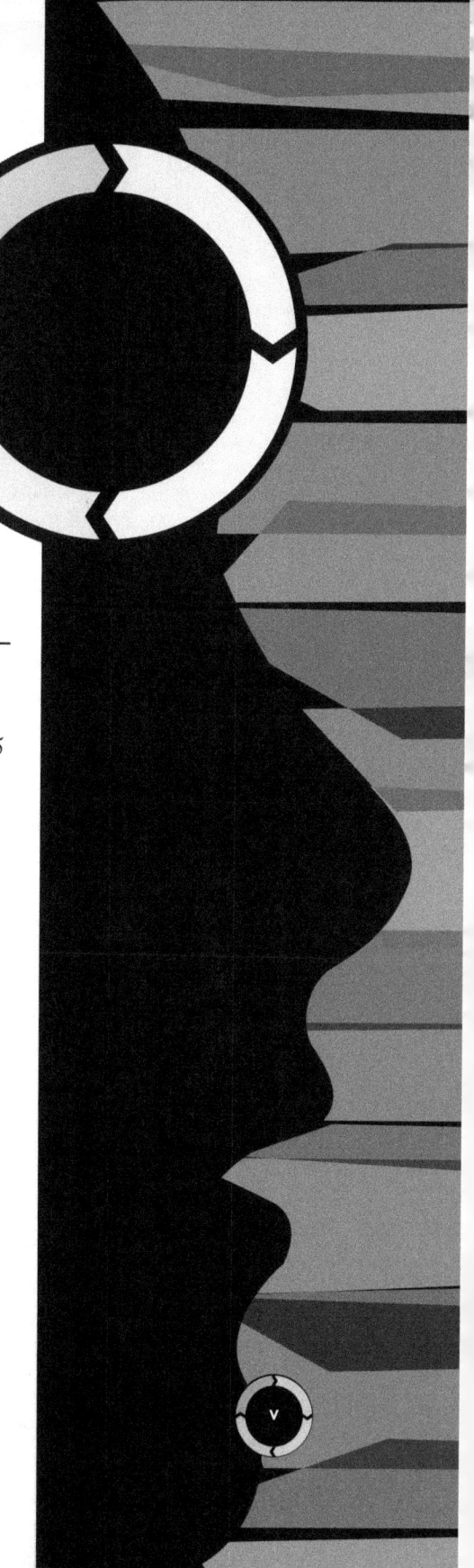

Preface ix
About the Authors xiv
Acknowledgements xvii
Introduction xix

CHAPTER 1 Liberal Arts: The Meaning and Purpose of General Education 1

What Is the *Meaning* and *Purpose* of the Liberal Arts? 1
The Liberal Arts Curriculum 4
Major Bodies of Knowledge in the Liberal Arts Curriculum 5
    Humanities 6
    Fine Arts 6
    Mathematics 7
    Natural Sciences 7
    Social and Behavioral Sciences 8
    Physical Health and Wellness 9
How the Liberal Arts Liberate You from Narrowness and Broaden Your Perspectives 12
The Social–Spatial Perspective: Beyond the Self to the Wider World 14
    The Perspective of Family 14
    The Perspective of Community 14
    The Perspective of Society 15
    The National Perspective 16
    The International Perspective 17
    The Global Perspective 18
    The Perspective of the Universe (Cosmos) 19
The Chronological Perspective: Embracing the Past, Present, and Future 19

      Historical Perspective 20
      Contemporary Perspective 20
      Futuristic Perspective 20
The Liberal Arts Liberate Development of the *Whole Person* 22
The Co-Curriculum: Using the *Whole Campus* to Develop the *Whole Person* 26
The Synoptic Perspective: Integrating the Multiples Perspectives of the Liberal Arts into a Coherent Whole 29
The Liberal Arts Develop Transferable Skills That Can Be Applied in Multiple Contexts 30
Internet Resources 33
Chapter Summary and Highlights 33
Questions and Final Reflections 35

CHAPTER 2 Benefits of the Liberal Arts 37

Broadening Your Personal Interests and Strengthening Social Self-Confidence 38
Developing the Capacity to Learn More Effectively and Efficiently 38
Thinking Critically from Multiple Perspectives 40
Thinking Creatively 42
Exploring and Selecting College Majors and Career Options 42
Acquiring Skills for Success in Your College Major 45
Enhancing Your Career Preparation and Career Success 48
Increasing Your Career Options and Occupational Versatility 53
Strengthening Your Prospects for Career Advancement and Leadership 55
Educating You for Life 56
Internet Resources 62
Chapter Summary and Highlights 62
Questions and Final Reflections 65

CHAPTER 3 The Meaning and Purpose of Diversity 67

What Is Diversity? 67
What Is Racial Diversity? 69

Humanity, Diversity, and the Liberal Arts: Foundation of a College Education

What Is Cultural Diversity? 73
What Is an Ethnic Group? 76
The Relationship between Diversity and Humanity 79
What Is Individuality? 82
What Is Ethnocentrism? 84
What Is Stereotyping? 86
What Is Prejudice? 88
What Is Discrimination? 89
Internet Resources 95
Chapter Summary and Highlights 96
Questions and Final Reflections 98

CHAPTER 4 The Relationship between Liberal Arts and Diversity 101

Diversity Advances and Enriches the Liberal Arts 101
Diversity Expands and Enriches the Multiple Perspectives
   Developed by the Liberal Arts 105
        Diversity and the Perspective of Self 105
        Diversity and the Perspective of Family 106
        Diversity and the Perspective of Community 107
        Diversity and the Perspective of Society 109
        Diversity and the National Perspective 109
        Diversity and the International Perspective 110
        Diversity and the Global Perspective 111
        Diversity and the Universe (Cosmos) 111
        Diversity and the Chronological Perspective 113
        Diversity and the Historical Perspective 113
        Diversity and the Contemporary Perspective 116
        Diversity and the Futuristic Perspective 119
Diversity Magnifies the Benefits of Liberal Arts 120
        Diversity Broadens Your Personal Interests and Builds
          Social Self-Confidence 120
        Diversity Accelerates and Deepens Learning 121
        Diversity Strengthens the Liberal Arts' Capacity to
          Promote Critical Thinking from Multiple
          Perspectives 122

    Diversity Stimulates Creative Thinking 124
    Diversity Enhances Career Preparation and Career Success 125
Internet Resources 127
Chapter Summary and Highlights 128
Questions and Final Reflections 130

CHAPTER 5 Tying It All Together: Developing a Plan for Making the Most of the Liberal Arts and Diversity 131

Developing a General Education Plan for Making the Most of the Liberal Arts 132
Developing an Action Plan for Infusing Diversity into Your College Experience 147
Strategies for Increasing Personal Contact and Interpersonal Interaction with Members of Diverse Groups 150
Tying It Altogether: Reflecting on Your College Experiences 159
Internet Resources 163
Chapter Summary and Highlights 164
Questions and Final Reflections 167

APPENDIX 171

REFERENCES 187

Preface

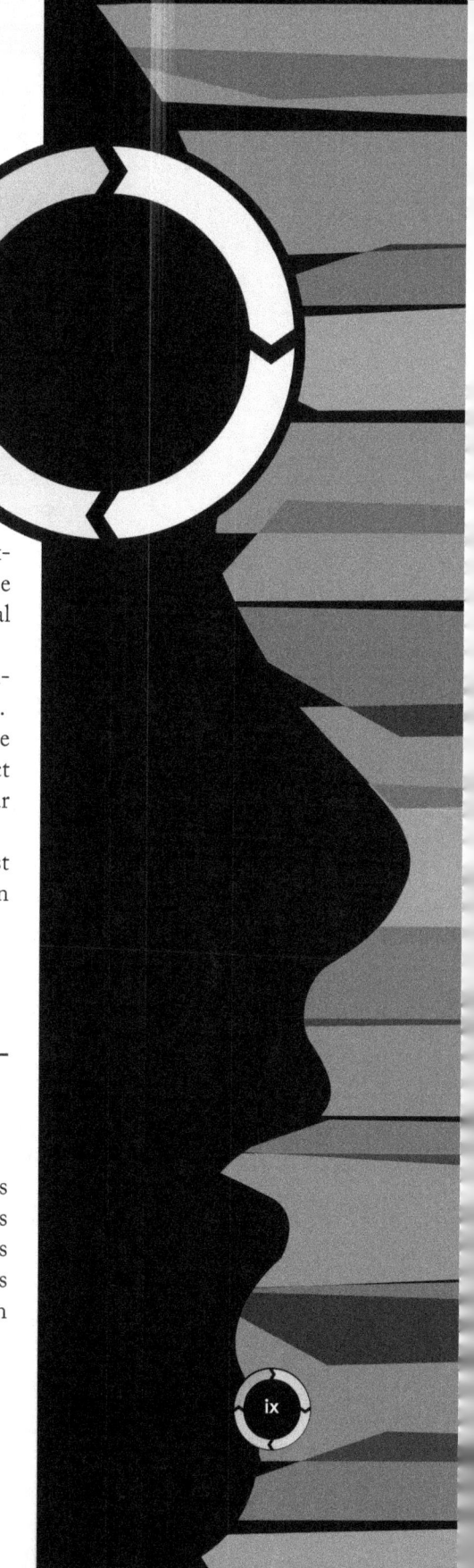

Purpose and Plan of This Book

The primary purposes of this book are to:

- Inform and excite you about your upcoming college experience, particularly the part that you will experience most intensively during your first two years: the liberal arts and general education.
- Explain how infusing diversity into the liberal arts will enrich the quality of your education and career preparation.
- Give you a sense of the "big picture"—an overview of the total college experience that will enable you to connect general education, your major, your electives, and your career.
- Help you create a long-range plan for making the most of your college experience and maximizing its impact on your future success.

Preview of Content

Chapter 1. Liberal Arts: The Meaning and Purpose of General Education

In this chapter, you will learn how general education broadens your perspective on the whole world and helps you develop as a whole person. This chapter also explains how the liberal arts provide the foundation on which all academic specializations (majors) are built, and how it provides vital skills for success in any occupation you may choose to pursue.

Chapter 2. Benefits of the Liberal Arts

Chapter 1 addresses the "what" question: What is general education? Chapter 2 addresses the "so what" question: *Why* is general education essential for success in college and beyond? This chapter identifies and documents the multiple benefits of the liberal arts, such as social self-confidence, deep learning, critical and creative thinking, exploring college majors, career preparation, and education for life.

Chapter 3. The Meaning and Purpose of Diversity

This chapter clarifies what "diversity" actually means, how it benefits all people, and how it is an integral element of a liberal arts education that enhances learning, self-awareness, and career development. The chapter also explains how the liberal arts equip students with the critical thinking skills needed to combat biased, ethnocentric thinking that undermines diversity and underlies stereotypes, prejudice, and discrimination.

Chapter 4. The Relationship between Liberal Arts and Diversity

This chapter explains how learning about and from diversity increases the power of the liberal arts. Exposure to different disciplines in the liberal arts curriculum opens your mind to multiple perspectives; so, too, does exposure to the different cultures and dimensions of diversity. Infusing diversity into the liberal arts enables you to appreciate the common themes that unite humans (humanity) along with the cultural variations on those themes (diversity). The chapter also lays out the multiple, practical advantages of integrating the liberal arts and diversity, such as improved performance in your chosen major and future career, increased self-awareness and self-confidence, and preparation for multiple life roles beyond college.

Chapter 5. Tying It All Together: Developing a Plan for Making the Most of the Liberal Arts and Diversity

This chapter helps you develop a plan for general education that amplifies the power of the liberal arts and the impact of a college education. You will learn how to use liberal arts courses strategically to test your interests and talents in fields that you might choose as a major (or minor), while simultaneously fulfilling general education requirements for graduation. The chapter also addresses myths about the relationship between liberal arts majors and careers, how co-curricular experiences are important career-building experiences, and how the quality of your college experience is magnified by infusing diversity into your educational plan.

Appendix

Acquiring knowledge is just the first step in the deep-learning process. The next step is to translate that knowledge into prudent and productive action—which is wisdom. This section of the book includes action-oriented exercises relating to each of the five chapters, including self-assessment plans for developing your "whole self" and for gaining self-awareness of your group identities, critical thinking attributes, and global-citizenship characteristics. The appendix concludes with a detailed action plan for incorporating the liberal arts and diversity into your college experience plan in a way that maximizes their impact on your personal development and future success.

Process and Style of Presentation

How instruction is delivered (the process) is as important as what information is delivered (the content). When writing this book, we made an intentional attempt to infuse the content with the following principles of deep learning.

Pause for Thought

At the *start* of each chapter, a question is posed to activate your thoughts and feelings about the chapter topic. This pre-reading exercise is designed to "warm up" or "tune up" your brain, preparing it to connect the ideas you're about to encounter with the ideas you already have in your head. It's an instructional strategy that implements one of the most powerful principles of human learning: humans learn most effectively when they relate what they're trying to learn to what they already know.

Additional pauses for thought are interspersed throughout each chapter that prompt you to reflect on the material you've just read. These timely pauses keep you mentally active throughout the reading process, serving to break up the reading process and break down the "attention drift" that normally builds up when the brain continually processes information for an extended period of time—as it does when reading.

These pauses for thought also deepen your understanding of the material because they encourage you to write about what you've read. Writing in response to reading promotes deeper thinking and more active learning than simply underlining or highlighting sentences.

Research and Scholarly Support

The book's ideas and recommendations are grounded in research and scholarship drawn from a variety of academic fields. You will find references cited regularly throughout the chapters and a sizable reference section at the end of the book. The sheer quantity of references cited serves as testimony to the fact that the subject matter of this book is built on a solid body of research and scholarship, just like any other academic subject studied in the college curriculum. You'll also find that the references include a balanced blend of older, "classic" scholarship and more recent "cutting edge" research. The wide range of academic fields and time periods reflected in the reference section serves to highlight the universal and timeless relevance of the ideas discussed in this book.

Multiple Modes of Sensory Input

Information in the chapters is delivered through a variety of formats, which includes diagrams, pictures, images, and concept maps. Inputting information into your brain through different sensory channels enables it to store that information in multiple places—which, in turn, deepens learning and strengthens memory.

Box Summaries

Throughout the book, you'll find boxes containing succinct summaries of key concepts and strategies. These boxed summaries pull together ideas relating to the same concept and organize them in the same physical place (on the page); this will help you to organize them in the same mental place (in your brain).

Key Points

Periodically, you will come across a highlighted phrase titled, "Key Point." This is a flag or cue indicating that the point being made deserves special attention and retention.

Sidebar Quotes

In the side margins of the book, you'll find quotes from famous and influential people that relate to and reinforce ideas being discussed at that point in the chapter. These quotes come from accomplished individuals who have lived in different historical periods and who have been successful leaders in a wide variety of fields—such as politics, philosophy, religion, science, business, music, art, and athletics. Also included among the sidebar quotes are the words of college students and college graduates. Studies show that students can learn much from other students—especially from students who've "been there, done that" and have experienced what you are about to experience.

Author's Experience

In each chapter you will find personal experiences shared by the authors. The authors share these with you for the purpose of personalizing the book and with the hope that you'll learn from their experiences as college professors, academic advisors, and former college students themselves—including their mistakes!

Internet Resources

At the end of each chapter, you will find websites for additional information relating to the chapter's major ideas. If the material presented in the chapter stimulates your interest and motivation to learn more about the topic, you can use the online resources cited at the end of the chapter to quickly access additional information.

End-of-Chapter Questions and Final Reflections

At the end of each chapter are questions and short exercises that encourage you to reflect on key concepts discussed in the chapter. These end-of-chapter reflections are designed to help deepen your understanding of these key concepts and "consolidate" them—that is, lock them into long-term memory.

About the Authors

Joe Cuseo holds a doctoral degree in Educational Psychology and Assessment from the University of Iowa and is Professor Emeritus of Psychology at Marymount College (California), where for more than 25 years he directed the first-year seminar (The Art of Being Human)—a core course required of all new students. He is a 14-time recipient of the "faculty member of the year award"—a student-driven award based on effective teaching and academic advising, the "Outstanding First-Year Student Advocate Award" from the National Resource Center for The First-Year Experience and Students in Transition, and the "Diamond Honoree Award" from the American College Personnel Association (ACPA) for contributions made to student development and the Student Affairs profession. Currently, Joe serves as an educational advisor and consultant for AVID—a non-profit organization whose mission is to promote the college access and success of underserved student populations.

Joe has delivered hundreds of campus workshops and conference presentations across North America, as well as Europe, Asia, Australia, and the Middle East. He's authored articles, monographs, and books on effective teaching, academic advising, student learning, and student success, the most recent of which are *Thriving in College and Beyond: Research-Based*

Strategies for Academic Success and Personal Development, Diversity and the College Experience, and *Peer-to-Peer Leadership: Transforming Student Culture.*

Aaron Thompson is the Executive Vice President and Chief Academic Officer for the Kentucky Council on Postsecondary Education. He is also a Professor of Sociology in the Department of Educational Leadership and Policy Studies at Eastern Kentucky University. Thompson holds a Ph.D. in Sociology in areas of Organizational Behavior and Race and Gender Relations. He has over 25 years of leadership experience in higher education and business. In addition, he has spent numerous years serving on non-profit boards in leadership roles. Throughout his career, Dr. Thompson has researched, taught and/or consulted in areas of diversity, leadership, ethics, multicultural families, race and ethnic relations, student success, first-year students, retention, cultural competence, and organizational design. He has over 30 publications and numerous research and peer-reviewed presentations. He has traveled over the United States and has given more than 700 workshops, seminars, and invited lectures in areas of race and gender diversity, living an unbiased life, overcoming obstacles to success, creating a school environment for academic success, cultural competence, workplace interaction, leadership, organizational goal setting, building relationships, the first-year seminar, and a variety of other topics. He has been and continues to be a consultant to educational institutions (elementary, secondary, and postsecondary), corporations, non-profit organizations, police departments, and other governmental agencies. His latest authored or co-authored books are *The Sociological Outlook, Infusing Diversity and Cultural Competence into Teacher Education,* and *Peer-to-Peer Leadership: Transforming Student Culture.* He also co-authored *Thriving in College and Beyond: Research-Based Strategies for Academic Success, Thriving in the Community College and Beyond: Research-Based Strategies for Academic Success and Personal Development, Diversity and the College Experience, Focus on Success,* and *Black Men and Divorce.*

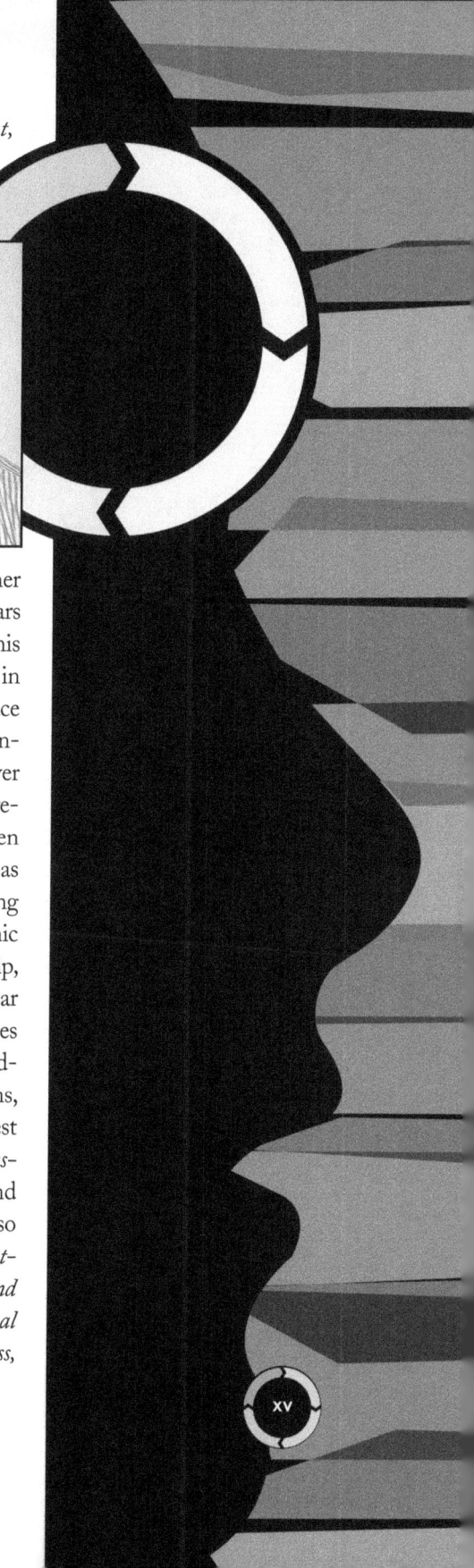

Acknowledgments

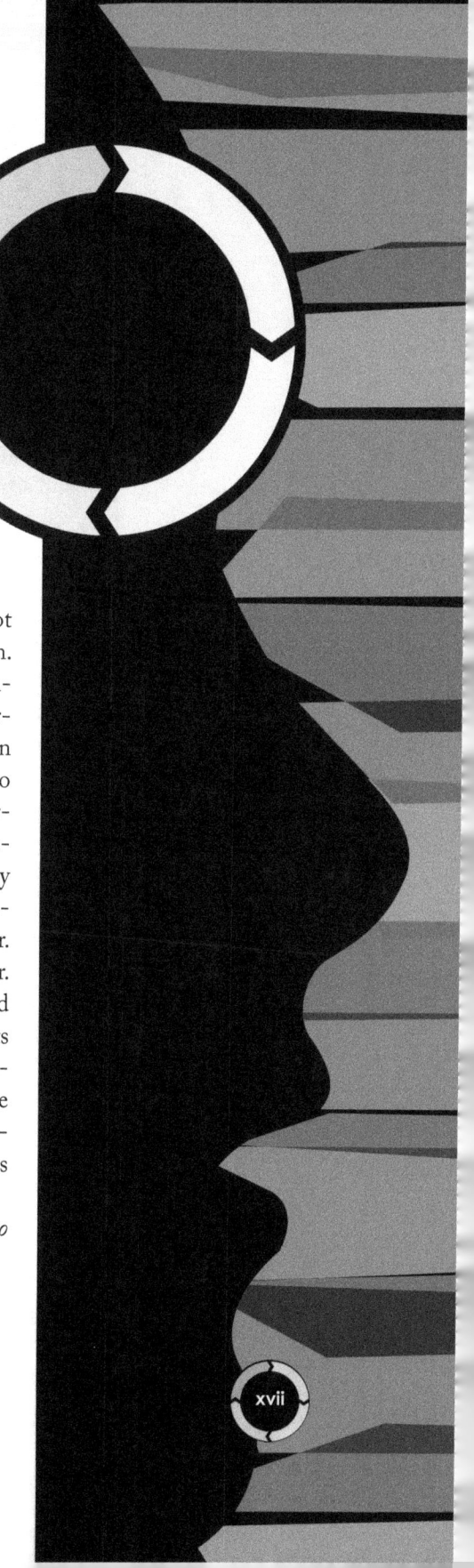

This book would never have been written if it were not for the influence of the people I'm about to mention. First and foremost, I thank the late Dr. Thomas Denver Wood, founding president of Marymount College (California), for teaching me about the dangers of narrow specialization ("doctoritis" as he derisively described it) and for alerting me to the practical power of the liberating arts ("education for survival" as he liked to call it). Thanks also to my esteemed faculty colleagues with whom I've shared many cross-disciplinary conversations in our common office wing and many interdisciplinary team-teaching experiences over the years, namely Dr. Charles Dock (biology), Dr. Pam Schachter (sociology), Dr. John Perkins (philosophy), Dr. Allen Franz (anthropology), and Dr. Nancy Sanders (English and Literature). This book reflects more than a quarter-of-a-century's worth of professional experiences at an authentically student-centered college where the liberal arts were delivered in a way that fostered deep appreciation of human differences (diversity) and authentic awareness of human unity (humanity).

Joe Cuseo

My Leadership Statement posted on my office wall states: "I believe that through study and life experience, individuals have opportunities to enrich their knowledge and refine their attitudes which are essential in acting responsibly. I believe in social justice and value those willing to utilize their talents assisting others in obtaining equitable justice. I believe in exercising power appropriately and strive to view all items in a critical and creative manner . . . ." These are my core values and they would not exist without a strong educational base in the liberal arts. There have been many individuals (so many that I cannot name them all) who assisted me in obtaining that base, especially in the area of understanding the importance of deep thinking and articulating my thoughts through the spoken and written word. It was my mother who first who sat me down and taught me the value of listening, thinking, writing, and speaking. One of her favorite expressions was: "Boy, you have two ears and one mouth, listen twice more than you speak." Many teachers like Donna Roberts (my high school senior English and speech teacher and school newspaper advisor) and college professors like Dr. Reid Luhman (sociology), Dr. Edith Williams (English), Dr. Frank Williams (philosophy), and Dr. Doris Wilkerson (one of my Ph.D. advisors) reinforced my mother's original message.

A liberal arts education is an education that keeps on giving. This is still clear today in my life with writing partners like Joe, who has a wonderful intellect and great humor meshed with superior thinking skills and creative ways to express those in written and verbal form. Thanks, Joe, for the opportunity to share our love of the liberal arts and how diversity is woven within them.

Aaron Thompson

Humanity, Diversity, and the Liberal Arts: Foundation of a College Education

Introduction

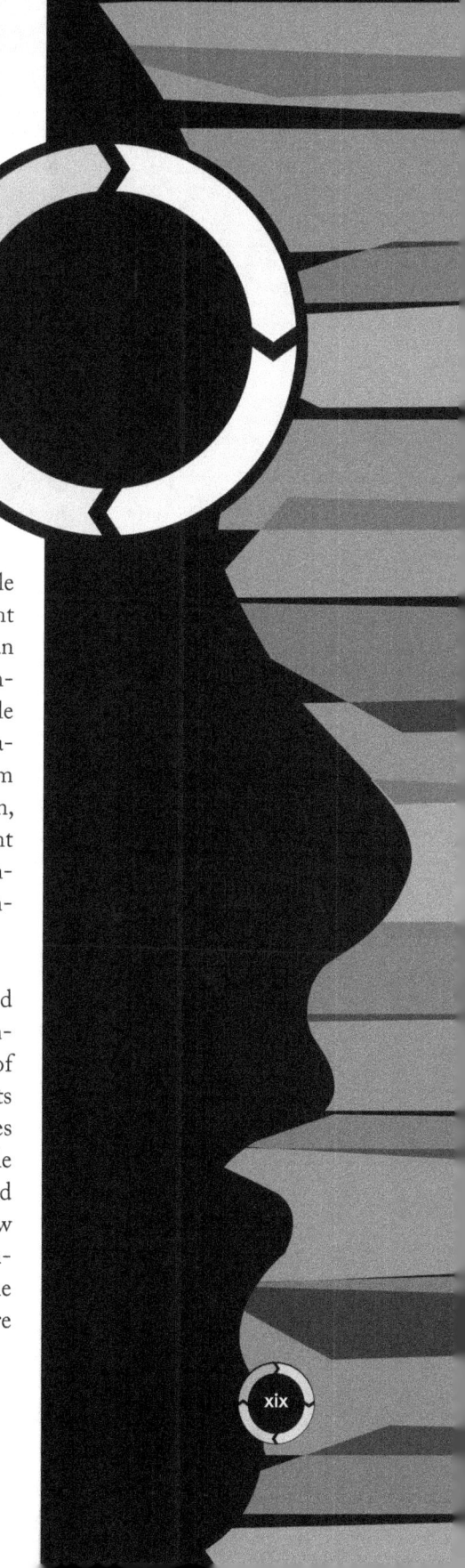

The "Blind Men and the Elephant" is an old Indian parable about a group of blind men who decided to touch an elephant to get an idea of what the animal looked like. One blind man touched the elephant's trunk, another touched the tail, and another touched the torso, but none of them touched the whole elephant. When the blind men got together to discuss the nature of the elephant, they all disagreed because each of them reached a conclusion that was based (and biased) by his own, egocentric perspective—that is, the single part of the elephant he experienced. None of the men had the broad, comprehensive perspective needed to get an integrated and complete understanding of the elephant.

If the elephant represented a college education and the blind men were college students, this book would function as a compass to guide students toward experiencing all the key parts of a college education and as a lynchpin to connect those parts into a unified whole. Said in another way, this book provides you with the "big picture"—a look at what the jigsaw puzzle should look like when it's completed—before you get involved (or get lost) assembling its individual pieces. It articulates how the liberal arts—the broad set of courses you'll take predominantly during the first two years of college—will provide the context and framework you need to make sense of your entire college experience.

The book also explains how the benefits of the liberal arts are expanded when they're infused with diversity. Learning about and from diverse cultures and people further extends the mind-expanding influence of the liberal arts, enabling you to view issues and solve problems from multiple perspectives. Similar to how your experiences with different disciplines (academic fields) in the liberal arts serve to liberate you from narrow, egocentric (self-centered) thinking, so do experiences with diverse cultural perspectives liberate you from the tunnel vision of ethnocentric (single culture-centered) thinking. The liberal arts and diversity complement one another, working together to empower you to detect common themes (humanity) and variations on those themes (diversity). They also combine to supply you with the skills needed to succeed in today's increasingly multicultural and globally interdependent world. Breadth of knowledge, flexible thinking skills, a cross-cultural perspective, and intercultural competence are essential skills for personal and professional success in the twenty-first century. These are the very skills developed by the liberal arts and diversity.

Surveys show that college students (and their parents) are preoccupied with specific majors and careers, and overlook, underrate, or underestimate the importance of general education. They tend to misinterpret the liberal arts as something political (leaning to the left) or impractical (having little to do with the "real world" and getting a real "real job"). Consequently, students often view liberal arts courses as unnecessary requirements they must "get out of the way" before they "get into" what's really important—their specialized major and specific career. This negative perception probably stems from two sources: (1) lack of knowledge about what the liberal arts actually stand for and are designed to do, and (2) misinterpretation of general education—a term often used interchangeably with the liberal arts—to mean something very "general" (non-specific) and without any particular value or practical purpose. This book debunks these myths with hard evidence and arguments that support the practical benefits of the liberal arts—for your major, your career, and your personal life; it also shows you how you can capitalize on and articulate these benefits to promote your success beyond college.

You are now on an educational journey of a lifetime. Compared to your previous school experiences, college will provide you with a wider range of course choices, more available resources available to support your development, and more freedom to determine your own educational direction. You can seize this opportunity to plan, shape, and create a college experience and a final college transcript that is uniquely your own. A well-planned college education that's intentionally infused with the liberal arts and diversity can serve as the seeds for lifelong growth. By planning to plant these seeds early and strategically, you can ensure that your investment in college yields the greatest growth. This book is designed to help you create and execute such a plan.

It could be said that your life after college will follow a pattern similar to that of the Chinese bamboo tree. The first four years of this tree's growth takes place underground, after which it emerges and grows as high as eighty feet. Similarly, your four years in college—especially if grounded in the liberal arts and diversity—provide the underlying seeds and roots for a lifelong growth. We hope that growth continues until you reach and surpass your tallest dreams.

Sincerely,
Joe Cuseo and Aaron Thompson

Liberal Arts
The Meaning and Purpose of General Education

PAUSE FOR THOUGHT

Before you start reading this chapter, please answer the following question: Which one of the following statements do you think represents the most accurate meaning of the term *liberal arts*?
1. Learning to be more artistic
2. Learning about things that are theoretical rather than practical
3. Learning to be less politically conservative
4. Learning to be a liberal spender
5. Learning skills for freedom

(The answer to this question will appear later in the chapter.)

What Is the *Meaning* and *Purpose* of the Liberal Arts?

If you are uncertain about the meaning of the term "liberal arts," you're not alone. Most college students don't have a clear idea about what the liberal arts actually represent (141). If they were to guess, they might mistakenly say it's "learning for its own sake" (144), or that is has something to do with liberal politics—as illustrated by the following true story.

Author's Experience—Joe Cuseo

I was once advising a student (Laura) who was majoring in business. While helping her develop a plan for graduation, I informed her that she needed to take a course in philosophy because it was a required part of our liberal arts curriculum. After I made this point, here's how our conversation went.

> **Laura** (in a somewhat irritated tone): Why do I have to take philosophy? I'm a business major.
> **Dr. Cuseo**: Because philosophy is an important part of a liberal arts education.
> **Laura** (in a very agitated tone): I'm not liberal and I don't want to be liberal! I'm conservative and so are my parents; we all voted for Ronald Reagan in the last election.

Laura probably would have picked option 1 as her answer to the multiple-choice question posed at the start of this chapter; she would have been wrong because the correct choice is option 5. Literally translated, the term "liberal arts" derives from two Latin words: liberalis—*meaning to "liberate" or "free," and* artes—*meaning "skills" (164). Thus, liberal arts mean "skills for freedom."*

The roots of the liberal arts date back to the origin of modern civilization—to the ancient Greeks and Romans who created a democratic republic in which citizens are given the freedom to elect their own leaders, thereby liberating them from uncritical dependence on an autocrat or dictator (35). Citizens of a democracy need to be skilled in the arts of critical thinking and persuasive communication in order to make wise choices about whom they elect as leaders and lawmakers, as well as to participate effectively in the democratic process. A liberal arts education was designed to supply them with these "skills for freedom" (144).

The political ideals of the ancient Greeks and Romans were shared by the founding fathers of the United States who also emphasized the importance of an educated citizenry for attaining and sustaining America's new democracy. James Madison, co-signer of the American Constitution and first author of the Bill of Rights, wrote: "Knowledge will forever govern ignorance; and a people who mean to be their own governors must arm themselves with the power which knowledge gives." Similarly, Thomas Jefferson, principal author of the United States Declaration of Independence, stated: "If a nation expects to be ignorant and free, it expects what never was and never will be."

Thus, the liberal arts are rooted in the belief that education and freedom are intertwined processes (278). Citizens educated in the liberal arts are empowered with the breadth of knowledge, depth of thinking, and communication skills that enable them to vote wisely and argue persuasively. To this day, the liberal arts continue to be a distinctive feature of the American college and university system, differentiating it from other educational systems around the world (76).

> "It is such good fortune for people in power that people do not think."
>
> —Adolf Hitler, German dictator

KEY POINT

The original purpose of college education in America was not just career preparation; it was preparation for citizenship and leadership in a democratic nation.

Over time, the original purpose of the liberal arts expanded to take on the more general meaning of liberating people to become self-directed critical thinkers capable of making decisions governed by well-reasoned ideas and values (112,155)—rather than by blind obedience to authority or social conformity. In addition to resisting manipulation by dictatorial politicians, self-directed critical thinkers are also able to resist manipulation by other societal forces, including:

- **Authority figures**—resisting excessive use or abuse of authority by parents, teachers, or law enforcers;
- **Peers**—resisting negative forms of social conformity and peer pressure; and
- **Media**—detecting and rejecting manipulative advertisements and misleading messages.

> "Advertisers rely on a half-educated public... because such people are easy to deceive with an effective set of logical and psychological tricks."
>
> —Robert Harris, *On the Purposes of a Liberal Arts Education*

CHAPTER 1: Liberal Arts: The Meaning and Purpose of General Education

In short, the liberal arts empower you to become a well-informed citizen and critical thinker who is armed and ready to ask the question: "Why?" It's the component of your college education that equips you with an inquiring mind and the mental tools to think independently.

The Liberal Arts Curriculum

Based on the educational philosophy of the ancient Greeks and Romans, the first liberal arts curriculum (collection of courses) originated during the Middle Ages and consisted of the following subjects: Logic, Language, Rhetoric (the art of argumentation and persuasion), Music, Mathematics, and Astronomy (16, 18, 247). The curriculum was designed to supply students with (1) a broad base of knowledge so they would be well informed in variety of subjects and (2) a flexible set of thinking skills for thinking deeply and critically about any subject.

The range of courses offered by today's colleges and universities is much broader than the original seven subjects that comprised the medieval curriculum. However, the original goal of the liberal arts curriculum has withstood the test of time; its primary purpose continues to be that of exposing students to a broad base of knowledge in multiple subject areas and equipping them with transferable thinking and communication skills that can be applied across different issues and situations (144).

Today, the liberal arts curriculum is sometimes referred to as *general education* to capture the fact that it supplies students with general knowledge and skills rather than narrow, specialized knowledge associated with a specific major or career. General education is what all college students learn, regardless of what their particular major or specialized field of study happens to be (16).

The liberal arts are also referred on some campuses as either (1) the *core curriculum*—what is central or essential for all students to learn, or (2) *breadth requirements*—representing a broad range of subject areas and skill sets.

Whatever term is used to describe the liberal arts on your campus, the bottom line is that they provide the foundation of a college education on which all academic specializations (majors) are built. The liberal arts signify what all college graduates should know and be able to do in order to succeed in any occupational path they choose to pursue.

PAUSE FOR THOUGHT

On your campus, what term(s) are used to refer to the subjects that all students must take in order to graduate?

KEY POINT

The liberal arts are what distinguish a college education from vocational training; they define what it means to be a well-educated person.

Major Bodies of Knowledge in the Liberal Arts Curriculum

The divisions of knowledge comprising today's liberal arts curriculum have expanded well beyond the seven subjects found in the original curriculum of medieval universities and vary somewhat from campus to campus. Variation across campuses also exists in terms of the specific courses that students are required to complete within each of these divisions of knowledge as well as the range of courses students can choose from to fulfill their general education requirements. Despite campus-to-campus variation in the exact number and nature of courses required for general education, the liberal arts curriculum on every college and university continues to represent the foundational knowledge and essential skills all college graduates should possess.

CHAPTER 1: Liberal Arts: The Meaning and Purpose of General Education

What follows is a description of the general divisions of knowledge and specific subject areas that make up the liberal arts curriculum on most campuses today. As you read the subject areas included in each of these divisions of knowledge, highlight those subjects in which you've never had a course.

Humanities

Courses in the Humanities division of the liberal arts focus on the human experience and the "big questions" that humans have always tried to answer, such as "Why are we here?" "What is the purpose of our existence?" "What does it mean to be human?" "How should we live?" "What is the good life?" and "Is there life after death?" Following are the primary subjects that comprise the Humanities, and the type of skills these subjects are designed to develop.

> "Challenging the meaning of life is the truest expression of the state of being human."
>
> —Viktor Frankl, Austrian neurologist, psychiatrist, and Holocaust survivor

- **Philosophy**—thinking rationally, acquiring wisdom (the ability to use knowledge prudently), and living an ethical life
- **Literature**—reading critically and appreciating the artistic merit of different literary genres (e.g., novels, short stories, poems, plays, and essays)
- **English Composition**—writing clearly, critically, and persuasively
- **Speech**—speaking clearly, eloquently, and convincingly
- **Languages**—speaking, reading, and writing in languages other than one's native tongue
- **Theology**—studying how humans believe and express their faith in a transcendent (supreme) being

> "You think your pain and your heartbreak are unprecedented in the history of the world, but then you read. It was books that taught me that the things that tormented me the most were the very things that connected me with all the people who were alive, and who have ever been alive."
>
> —James Baldwin, African American novelist, essayist, playwright, and poet

Fine Arts

Courses in the Fine Arts division of the liberal arts focus largely on the art of human expression, asking such questions as "How do humans create, and appreciate what is beautiful?" and "How do humans express themselves aesthetically (through the senses), imaginatively, and stylistically?" Following are the primary subdivisions of the Fine Arts, and the type of skills these subjects are designed to develop.

Humanity, Diversity, and the Liberal Arts: Foundation of a College Education

- **Visual Arts**—expressing and appreciating creativity demonstrated through visual representation (drawing, painting, sculpture, photography, and graphic design)
- **Musical Arts**—expressing and appreciating creativity demonstrated through rhythmical arrangements of sounds
- **Performing Arts**—appreciating and expressing creativity through drama and dance

Mathematics

Courses in the Mathematics division of the liberal arts are designed to develop numerical skills, quantitative reasoning, and data analysis. Following are the subjects that typically comprise general education in mathematics, and the type of skills these subjects are designed to develop.

- **Algebra**—mathematical reasoning and logical thinking expressed through symbolic representation of numbers in the language of letters
- **Statistics**—mathematical methods for summarizing quantitative data; estimating probabilities; representing and understanding numerical information depicted in graphs, charts, and tables; and drawing accurate inferences from statistical data
- **Calculus**—advanced mathematical skills for calculating areas enclosed by curves and the rate at which the quantity of one entity changes in relation to another

Natural Sciences

Courses in the Natural Sciences division of the liberal arts curriculum focus on the systematic observation of the physical world and underlying explanations of natural phenomena, asking such questions as "What causes the physical events that take place in the natural world?" "How can we predict and control natural events?" "How do we promote harmonious interaction between humans and the natural environment to support their mutual survival and development?" Following are the primary subject areas that comprise the Natural Sciences, and the type of skills these subjects are designed to develop.

"Dancing is silent poetry."

—Simonides, ancient Greek poet

"The universe is a grand book which cannot be read until one learns to comprehend the language and become familiar with the characters of which it is composed. It is written in the language of mathematics."

–Galileo Galilei, seventeenth-century Italian physicist, mathematician, astronomer, and philosopher

"The media through which we get our information about the world are full of charts, graphs, and statistical information. Important decisions you will make about such matters as a medical treatment, home buying or voting will depend on your math skills."

—Robert Shoenberg, Senior Fellow, Association of American Colleges and Universities

> "There are in fact two things, science and opinion; the former begets knowledge, the latter ignorance."
>
> —Hippocrates, ancient Greek philosopher, physician, and the "father of western medicine"

- **Biology**—understanding the structure and underlying processes of all living things
- **Chemistry**—understanding the composition of natural and synthetic (man-made) substances, how these substances may be modified and how new substances can be developed
- **Physics**—understanding the properties of physical matter, its principles of energy and motion, and how they are affected by electrical and magnetic forces
- **Geology**—examining the composition of the earth and the natural processes that have shaped its development
- **Astronomy**—exploring the makeup and motion of celestial bodies that comprise the cosmos

Social and Behavioral Sciences

Courses in the Social and Behavioral Sciences division of the liberal arts focus on the systematic observation of human behavior, both individually and in groups, asking such questions as "What causes people to behave the way they do?" and "How can we predict, control, and improve the quality of human behavior and social interaction?" Following are subjects within this division of the liberal arts curriculum, and the type of skills these subjects are designed to develop.

- **History**—understanding past events, their causes, and their influence on current events
- **Political Science**—understanding how societal authority is organized and how this authority is exerted to govern people, make collective decisions, and maintain social order
- **Psychology**—understanding the human mind, its conscious and subconscious processes, and the underlying causes of human behavior
- **Sociology**—understanding how people behave in groups, organizations, and institutions that comprise human society (e.g., families, schools, health services, and corporations)
- **Anthropology**—understanding the cultural origins, physical origins, and development of the human species
- **Geography**—understanding how the place (physical location) where humans live shapes, and is shaped by, their culture

- **Economics**—understanding how the material needs of humans are met through allocation of limited resources and how monetary wealth is generated by societal production of goods and services as they are distributed, priced, and utilized

Physical Health and Wellness

Courses in the Physical Health and Wellness division of the liberal arts focus on the human body, how to maintain optimal health, and how to attain peak levels of human performance. They ask such questions as "How does the body function most effectively?" and "What can humans do to minimize illness, maximize wellness, and improve the overall quality of their lives?" Following are the primary subject areas comprising this division of the curriculum, and the type of skills these subjects are designed to develop.

- **Physical Education**—understanding the role of human exercise for maximizing health and promoting peak performance
- **Nutrition**—understanding how the body uses food as nourishment for maintaining health and as fuel for generating energy
- **Sexuality**—understanding the biological, psychological, and social aspects of sexual relations
- **Drug Education**—understanding how body-altering and mind-altering substances affect physical health, mental states, and human behavior

> "Man, the molecule of society, is the subject of social science."
>
> —Henry Charles Carey, nineteenth-century American economist

> "To eat is a necessity, but to eat intelligently is an art."
>
> —La Rochefoucauld, seventeenth-century French author

PAUSE FOR THOUGHT

Look back at the above mentioned subject areas of the liberal arts. For those subjects in which you've never had a course, identify a field of study that strikes you as personally interesting or potentially useful, and provide a brief explanation why.

> "In college ... you will be expected to get inside what you are learning to apply it, make comparisons and connections, draw implications, and use ideas."
>
> —Robert Shoenberg, author, *Why Do I Have to Take This Course?*

> "Science is a way of thinking much more than it is a body of knowledge."
>
> —Carl Sagan, American astronomer, astrophysicist, cosmologist, and Pulitzer Prize winner

Most of the liberal arts courses that students take to fulfill general education requirements will be taken during your first two years of college. Don't be dismayed if some of these requirements look similar to courses you had in high school. College courses in these subject areas will not be videotape replays of courses you've already taken; you will learn these subjects in greater depth and with higher levels of critical thinking than you did in high school (76). Research reveals that the greatest gains in learning and thinking that students make in college take place during their first two years (232)—the years when most liberal arts courses are taken.

The breadth of knowledge you acquire in the liberal arts allows you to stand on the shoulders of intellectual giants from a wide range of fields and capitalize on their collective wisdom. In addition to acquiring this broad base of knowledge, the liberal arts also discipline your mind to *think* in a variety of ways. This is why different academic divisions in college are often referred to as *disciplines*—by studying them, you begin to develop the "mental discipline" that faculty in these fields have spent years of their lives developing. For instance, when you study history, algebra, biology, and art, you are disciplining your mind to think chronologically (history), symbolically (algebra), scientifically (biology), and aesthetically (art).

The diverse subjects you encounter in the different divisions of the liberal arts will stretch your mind, giving you the intellectual flexibility to think in complementary ways, such as the following:

- Linguistically and numerically
- Concretely and abstractly
- Objectively and subjectively
- Imaginatively and symbolically
- Systematically—in deliberate step-by-step sequences, and intuitively—via sudden flashes of insight (93, 156)

These multiple ways of thinking and knowing serve to diversify your mental repertoire and deepen your knowledge of any concept you're studying (261). In addition, they enable you to think *critically* about any topic or issue you encounter in college and beyond. When you think critically, you raise the bar and jack up your thinking to levels that go beyond merely remembering, reproducing, or regurgitating factual information. "Education is what's left over after you've forgotten all the facts" is an old saying that carries a lot of truth because memory for factual information has a short lifespan. Studies show that students' memory of facts learned in college often fades with time (231, 232). However, learning to think at a higher level is a durable, lifelong learning skill that you retain forever (like learning to ride a bike).

Compared to high school, college courses focus less on memorizing information and focus more on thinking critically about issues, concepts, and principles (76). National surveys of college professors teaching freshman-level through senior-level courses in various fields reveal that more than 95 percent of them believe the most important goal of a college education is to develop students' ability to think critically (113, 194). Similarly, college professors teaching introductory courses to freshmen and sophomores indicate that the primary educational purpose of their courses is to develop students' critical thinking skills (142, 266). Simply stated, college instructors are often more concerned with teaching you *how* to think than with teaching you *what* to think (i.e., what facts to remember). **Box 1.1** contains a definition of critical thinking and its major forms.

Rafael Ramirez Lee/Shutterstock.com

CHAPTER 1: Liberal Arts: The Meaning and Purpose of General Education

> **BOX 1.1**
>
> **Forms of Critical Thinking**
>
> Critical thinking is a process of critiquing (evaluating) the quality of your thinking and the thinking of others. Following are the major thought processes to which critical thinking may be applied.
>
> **Analysis (analytical thinking)**—breaking down ideas and identifying their key components, underlying assumptions, or missing elements
>
> **Synthesis**—building up ideas by integrating them into a larger, more coherent organizational framework or system
>
> **Application (applied thinking)**—putting knowledge into practice to solve problems and resolve issues
>
> **Creative thinking**—generating and evaluating ideas that are unique, original, or innovative
>
> **Multidimensional thinking**—thinking about yourself and the world around you from different vantage points (e.g., different cultural or disciplinary perspectives)
>
> **Balanced thinking**—carefully considering arguments and evidence for/against opposing points of view by weighing their relative strengths and weaknesses

How the Liberal Arts Liberate You from Narrowness and Broaden Your Perspectives

In addition to developing your ability to think critically, the liberal arts ensure that your thinking is comprehensive and complete. The wide range of subjects you encounter in the liberal arts equip you with a wide-angle lens for viewing the world around you from a broader perspective (46). The key components of this broader perspective are organized and illustrated in **Figure 1.1**. The center circle in the figure represents the self. Fanning out to the right of the self is a series of increasingly wider arches that represent the broadening elements of a *social–spatial perspective*. This perspective takes you from micro to macro, expanding your view to include larger social groups and more distant places, ranging from the narrowest perspective (the individual) to the broadest perspective (the universe). This expanded social–spatial perspective provides you with a panoramic view of the world, enabling you to step outside yourself and see yourself in relation to other people and other places.

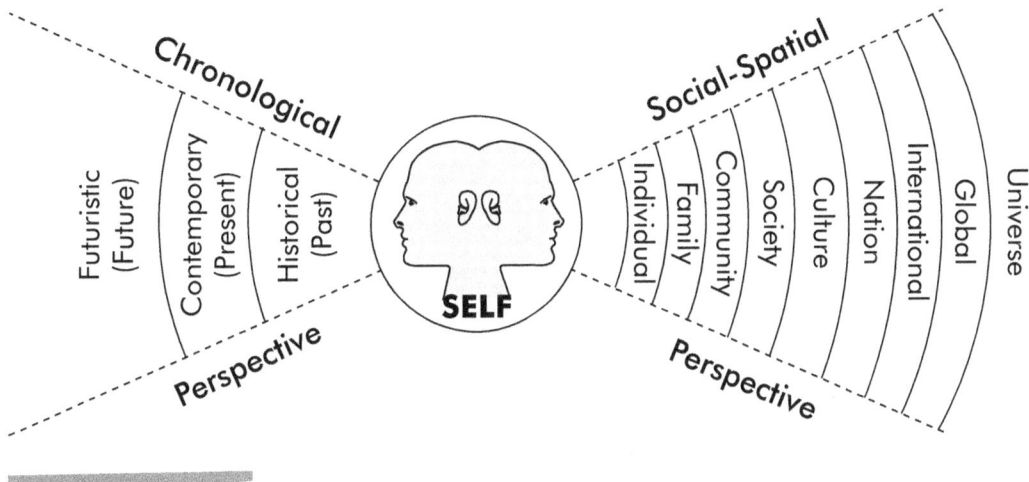

FIGURE 1.1 Multiple Perspectives Developed by the Liberal Arts

In Figure 1.1, to the left of the self are three arches that comprise the *chronological perspective*. This perspective embraces the three key dimensions of time: *past* (historical)—the way things were, *present* (contemporary)—the way things are, and *future* (futuristic)—the way things are likely to be. A chronological perspective gives you hindsight to see where the world has been, insight to see the world's current condition, and foresight to see where the world is going. It stretches your perspective beyond the here and now, enabling you to view yourself in relation to humans who have lived before you and humans who will live after you.

Thus, the social–spatial perspective widens your frame of reference and the chronological perspective lengthens it. Together, these two broadening perspectives developed by the liberal arts enable to you to appreciate the human experience of people living long ago and far away.

The Social–Spatial Perspective: Beyond the Self to the Wider World

When you develop a "world view," you take the perspective of (1) larger social units—moving from the individual (self) to larger groups of people, and (2) larger units of space—moving from local to distal. The components of this broadening social–spatial perspective are described next.

The Perspective of Family

One of the ways in which a liberal arts education broadens your perspective is by deepening your understanding of how the family influences human development. The people with whom you were raised have almost certainly shaped the person you are today. Moreover, just as family influences an individual, an individual can influence his or her family. For example, going to college is likely to influence your parents' view of you and may influence the decision of other members of your immediate or extended family to attend college. If you have children, your college experience will likely impact their development because research shows that children of college graduates experience improved intellectual development, better physical health, and greater economic security (44, 45, 231, 232).

The Perspective of Community

In addition to being nested in a family, you're also nested in a larger social unit—your community. A community may be defined as a group of people that share the same environment, interests, beliefs, and values (62). This circle of community members includes people in your local neighborhood, your school, and place of work. If you want to make the world a better place, this is where to start—by engaging in service and leadership in the communities where you live and work. As William Cronon notes: "In the act of making us free, it [liberal arts education] also binds us to the communities that gave us our freedom in the first place; it makes us responsible to those communities in ways that limit our freedom. In the end, it turns out that liberty is not about thinking or saying or doing whatever we want. It is about exercising our freedom in such a way as to make a difference in the world and make a difference for more than just ourselves" (80).

One way in which civic engagement can be demonstrated is by stepping beyond our narrow self-interests to volunteer time and energy to help members of our local community, particularly those in need. Engaged citizens demonstrate their humanity in two ways: (1) by being *humane*—through genuine compassion for others less fortunate than themselves, and (2) by being *humanitarian*—devoting time and effort to promote the welfare of other human beings. Civic engagement is one of the goals a college education and studies show that this goal is being achieved because college graduates demonstrate higher rates of participation in civic affairs and community service (44, 45, 232).

"Think globally, act locally."

—Patrick Geddes, Scottish urban planner and social activist

KEY POINT

A college education is not only about learning how to earn a better living; it's also about learning how to be a better human being.

The Perspective of Society

Moving beyond our local communities, we're also members of a larger *society*—a group of people organized under the same social system. A society includes subgroups of people from different geographic regions—north, south, east, west; population densities—urban, suburban, rural; and races or ethnicities—minority and majority groups.

Human societies also consist of groups of people stratified (divided) into different social classes with unequal amounts of resources and material wealth; those groups occupying lower social strata have less economic resources and social privilege (103). Level of education, personal income, and occupational prestige are the three key

> "It [a liberal arts education] shows you how to accommodate yourself to others, how to throw yourself into their state of mind, how to come to an understanding of them. You are at home in any society; you have common ground with every class."
>
> —John Henry Newman, *The Idea of a University*

criteria used to define one's social class or socioeconomic status (SES), and all three tend to be interrelated. For instance, young adults from high-income families are more than seven times likely to have earned a college degree and hold a prestigious position than those from low-income families (228).

These differences may be explained, at least in part, by the fact that young adults from families with higher income levels and socioeconomic status are privileged with two major forms of capital, each of which contributes to their higher rates of college attendance and college completion: (1) economic capital—the *material* resources they possess (e.g., homes, health benefits, discretionary income for travel, technology, tutors, and other enriching educational experiences for their children); and (2) social capital—*who* they know (43) (e.g., contacts with employers, college counselors, college admissions officials, and "power players" in the legal and political system).

A societal perspective helps us understand how such stratification has advantaged or disadvantaged us as individuals, and increases our empathy for less privileged members of our society.

The National Perspective

In addition to being members of a society, we are also citizens of a nation. Citizens in a democratic nation are expected to be informed and engaged participants in its system of governance—as voters—and in its judicial system—as jurors.

When there are low voter turnouts, citizens with more moderate political views are more likely not to vote, while people with more extreme views continue to vote. Thus, low turnouts can result in a more polarized political system that's less conducive to bipartisan negotiation and compromise. Also, when there are low voter turnouts, politicians are more likely to use extreme media tactics to recruit voters—such as attack ads and smear campaigns—to instill public fear of the opposing candidate (40).

It's noteworthy that American citizens between the ages of 18 and 24 have the lowest voter-turnout rate of any age group that's eligible to vote (82). If you're in this age group, don't contribute to this disturbing statistic. Remember that the right to vote is the hallmark of a democratic nation, and having the privilege of citizenship in a free nation brings with it the responsibility of learning about and participating in the country's governance through the voting process. "Civic responsibility must be learned, for it is neither natural nor effortless. It takes work to inform oneself sufficiently to cast an intelligent vote" (40). Recent surveys reveal that employers of college graduates feel the same way: 83 percent of them agree that college students should take classes that build civic knowledge and judgment (136).

> "Get involved. Don't gripe about things unless you are making an effort to change them. You can make a difference if you dare."
>
> —Richard C. Holbrooke, former director of the Peace Corps and American ambassador to the United Nations

Recall that a foundational purpose of the liberal arts is to educate citizens broadly and deeply, so they can vote wisely and ensure the quality of a democracy. The signers of the Declaration of Independence believed that the pursuit of personal happiness could not take place without pursuing the good of the nation, because the well-being of the whole and the well-being of the individual were inescapably interrelated (167).

KEY POINT

Don't forget that your investment in a college education is not only an investment in yourself, it's also an investment in your nation.

PAUSE FOR THOUGHT

Did you vote in the last presidential election? If yes, why? If no, why not?

The International Perspective

Moving beyond our particular country of citizenship, we're also members of an international world that includes close to 200 nations (252). Citizens in every nation today are affected by events that cross national borders; boundaries between nations are melting away as a

> "[College] graduates need to develop a sense of global citizenship ... to care about people in distant places, to understand the nature of global economic integration, to appreciate the interconnectedness and interdependence of people, and to protect planet Earth."
>
> —Yong Zhao, noted Chinese painter, calligrapher, and poet

result of increased international travel, international trading, and the growth of multinational corporations (111). In addition, rapid advances in electronic technology have created more opportunities for citizens of different nations to communicate with each other than at any other time in world history (95, 264). The World Wide Web (www) has made today's world "a small world after all" and success in it requires an international perspective. The liberal arts curriculum is intentionally designed to help you develop this perspective.

The Global Perspective

Even broader than an in international perspective is a global perspective. It extends beyond nations to embrace both human and nonhuman life inhabiting our planet and how these diverse life forms interface with the earth's natural resources (minerals, air, and water). Humans share the earth with approximately 10 million animal species (200) and more than 300,000 forms of vegetative life, all of whose needs must be met and balanced to ensure the health and sustainability of our planet (168). Just as we need to avoid egocentrism—thinking that the self is the center of the universe, we also need to avoid *anthropocentrism*—believing that we humans are the only significant life form on the planet while ignoring (or abusing) other elements of the natural world (125).

> "Treat the Earth well. It was not given to you by your parents. It was loaned to you by your children."
>
> —Kenyan proverb

A global perspective includes consideration of how humans' industrial and economic pursuits impact the earth's sustainability. As "global citizens" of the same planet, we have an environmental responsibility to address issues that threaten Mother Earth's natural resources and the life forms that depend on its resources for survival. Global research indicates that the earth's atmosphere is gradually thickening and trapping more heat as a result of a buildup in gases created by our burning fossil fuels for industrial purposes (148). The consensus among today's scientists is that this buildup of man-made pollution is causing temperatures to rise (and sometimes fall) around the world, resulting in more extreme weather conditions and more frequent natural disasters—such as droughts, wildfires, hurricanes, and dust storms (153, 213, 214). Addressing the issue of climate change requires a global perspective that appreciates how waste admissions generated on our planet need to be held within the planet's environmental capacity to sustain them (90, 120).

The Perspective of the Universe (Cosmos)

Beyond the global perspective is the broadest of all perspectives—the perspective of the universe. This cosmological perspective positions us to view earth as one planet sharing a solar system with multiple planets and as a single celestial body sharing a galaxy with millions of other celestial bodies that include stars, moons, meteorites, and asteroids (100).

It's noteworthy that astronomy was one of the seven essential subjects included in the original liberal arts curriculum developed during the Middle Ages. The timeless intrigue of the cosmos is supported by modern-day cosmologists who consider reflecting on the massive and mysterious nature of the universe—how it may have begun, where it may be going, and whether it will ever end—to be spiritual questions (301). Modern-day astronauts who have traveled beyond the earth's force of gravity to view the universe from the perspective of outer space have also described their expanded perspective as a "spiritual" experience.

Whether you view the universe through the physical telescope of astronomy or the spiritual scope of reflective contemplation, it qualifies as the broadest of all social–spatial perspectives developed by the liberal arts.

> "In astronomy, you must get used to viewing the earth as just one planet in the larger context of the universe."
>
> —Physics professor (93)

> "Man must rise above the Earth—to the top of the atmosphere and beyond—for only thus will he fully understand the world in which he lives."
>
> —Socrates, classic Greek (Athenian) philosopher a founding father of Western philosophy

The Chronological Perspective: Embracing the Past, Present, and Future

In addition to broadening your perspective of the world by equipping you with knowledge about other people and places, studying the liberal arts also stretches your perspective of time by enabling you to learn about the past and its relationship to the present and future. Following are the key dimensions of a chronological perspective.

> "A liberal [arts] education frees a person from the prison-house of class, race, time, place, background, family, and nation."
>
> —Robert Hutchins, former dean of Yale Law School and president of the University of Chicago

Historical Perspective

> "Those who cannot remember the past are damned to repeat it."
>
> —George Santayana, Spanish-born American philosopher

Humans are products of both their social and natural history. An historical perspective gives you insight into the root causes of the current human condition and world situation. We need to remember that the earth is estimated to be more than 4.5 billion years old and our human ancestors date back more than 250,000 years (168). Viewed from this perspective, the lifespan of humans living today represents just a very small frame of time in a very long chronological reel. Every modern convenience we now enjoy reflects the collective knowledge and cumulative effort of humans that have been amassed over thousands of years of history. By studying the past, we build on our ancestors' success and learn from their mistakes. We've built on the architectural knowledge of the Egyptian pyramid makers to construct more advanced buildings today, and by understanding the causes and consequences of the Holocaust, we reduce the risk that an atrocity of such size and scope will ever happen again.

Contemporary Perspective

A contemporary perspective gives us insight into the issues and events reported in the daily news. Critical thinking about current events is essential because contemporary television and internet-based news reporting has become more politically biased; political campaigns today also use more manipulative media advertisements—relying on short sound bites, one-sided arguments, and powerful visual images designed to appeal to emotions and discourage deep thinking (42, 118). Thus, the original goal of the liberal arts to develop knowledgeable, critical thinking citizens is as important today as any time in American history.

> "Yesterday is gone. Tomorrow has not yet come. We have only today. Let us begin."
>
> —Mother Teresa of Calcutta, Albanian, Catholic nun and winner of the Nobel Peace Prize

The liberal arts strengthen your understanding of the contemporary perspective and supply you with the skills and wisdom to improve it (133, 193).

Futuristic Perspective

A futuristic perspective frees us from the here and now, allowing us to envision what our world will be like years from now. This perspective focuses on confronting the future challenges facing humankind, asking such questions as "Will we leave the world a better place for those who will leave after our departure, including our children and grandchildren?" and "How can we avoid short-term, shortsighted thinking that only benefits out current lives and take a long-range perspective that enables us to anticipate the consequences of our current actions on future generations of humans?"

We need to be mindful that our individual lifespan is incredibly short when compared to the lifespan of humanity. Viewing humanity from extended perspective underscores our moral responsibility to use the limited time we have on earth to promote the quality and sustainability of life for future generations of humans.

To sum up, a comprehensive chronological perspective brings our view of the past, present, and future into focus on a single screen. It enables us to see how the current world is a short snippet in a much longer temporal sequence that has been shaped by past events and will shape future events. When you combine the dimensions of a comprehensive chronological perspective with the broad-based dimensions of a social–spatial perspective, you're able to unravel and understand the multiple layers of context within which specific issues in today's world are embedded. (These layers of context are illustrated in **Figures 1.2** and **1.3**.)

"The future is literally in our hands to mold as we like. But we cannot wait until tomorrow. Tomorrow is now."

—Eleanor Roosevelt, United Nations diplomat, humanitarian, and wife of President Franklin D. Roosevelt

"We all inherit the past. We all confront the challenges of the present. We all participate in the making of the future."

—Ernest Boyer and Martin Kaplan, *Educating for Survival*

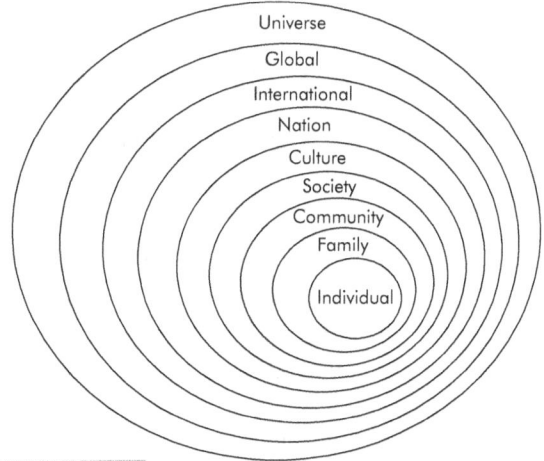

FIGURE 1.2 Nested Social–Spatial Perspectives: Interconnected People and Places

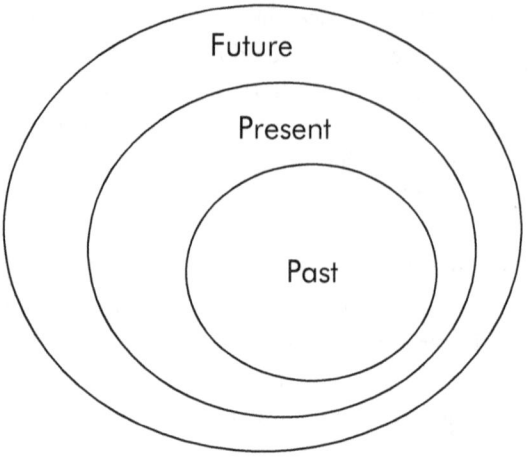

FIGURE 1.3 Nested Chronological Perspectives: Interconnected Times

PAUSE FOR THOUGHT

What historical event or development in your lifetime do you think is having the most impact on today's world and will continue to impact the world of the future?

The Liberal Arts Liberate Development of the *Whole Person*

"A liberal arts education can help us develop a more comprehensive understanding of the universe and ourselves."

—Spencer McWilliams, *Liberal Arts Education: What Does It Mean? What Is It Worth?*

In addition to expanding your knowledge of the world around you, the liberal arts expand your knowledge of the world within you. Well-educated people not only look outward to learn about the world around them, they also look inward to learn about themselves. Scholars consider introspection (the ability to inspect or examine yourself) to be a major form of human intelligence, referred to as "intrapersonal intelligence" (114, 115).

"Know thyself" was a famous exhortation issued by Socrates, the ancient and influential Greek philosopher. It is also one of the most frequently cited goals of a liberal arts education (81, 279). To know thyself—to be fully self-aware—requires knowledge of the *whole* self. The liberal arts liberate us from a narrow or single-dimensional view of ourselves, enabling us to become aware of the multiple components that comprise the "self."

As illustrated in **Figure 1.4,** the self is a multidimensional entity comprised of multiple identities, all of which are interrelated and interdependent. We are not just thinking (intellectual) beings or working (vocational) beings; we are also social, emotional, physical, ethical, and spiritual beings.

Know Thyself

Self-awareness is one of the most important outcomes of a liberal arts education.

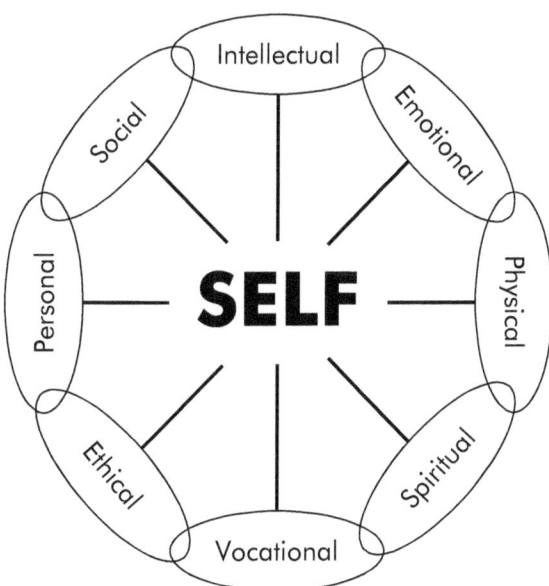

FIGURE 1.4 Key Elements of Holistic (Whole-Person) Development

> "Everyone is a house with four rooms: a physical, a mental, an emotional, and a spiritual. Most of us tend to live in one room most of the time but unless we go into every room every day, even if only to keep it aired, we are not complete."
>
> —Native American proverb

Comprehensive self-awareness and self-development embraces the following key components of self.

1. **Intellectual**—acquiring broad-based knowledge, learning how to learn, and learning how to think critically
2. **Emotional**—understanding, managing, and expressing emotions
3. **Social**—improving the quality and depth of interpersonal relationships
4. **Ethical (character) development**—developing a clear value system for guiding personal decisions, making sound ethical judgments, and demonstrating consistency between your convictions (beliefs) and your commitments (actions)
5. **Physical**—acquiring knowledge about the human body and applying that knowledge to prevent disease, preserve wellness, and promote peak performance
6. **Spiritual**—devoting attention to the "big questions" such as the meaning or purpose of life, the inevitability of death, and the origins of human life and the natural world
7. **Vocational**—exploring career options and pursuing a career path that is consistent with our talents, interests, and values
8. **Personal**—developing a strong sense of personal identity, a coherent self-concept, and capacity to manage personal affairs and resources

(For a more detailed description of these eight elements of self-development, see exercise for Chapter 1 in the Appendix.)

PAUSE FOR THOUGHT

Which one of the eight dimensions of self listed above are you most interested in developing in college? Why?

As can be seen in Figure 1.4, the different dimensions of self are interrelated. They do not operate independently but interdependently; they in-

Humanity, Diversity, and the Liberal Arts: Foundation of a College Education

tersect with each other to influence our personal development and overall well-being (160, 183). Our intellectual performance is influenced by our emotional state (e.g., whether we're enthusiastic or anxious); our emotional state is influenced by our social relationships (e.g., whether we feel lonely or loved); and our social relationships are influenced by our physical identity (e.g., whether we have a positive or negative body image). If one link in the chain is strengthened or weakened, other dimensions of the self are likely to be simultaneously strengthened or weakened. This ripple effect is supported by research on college students, which indicates that when they develop intellectually, they also develop higher levels of self-esteem and social self-confidence (231, 232).

National surveys show that the reason why most students go to college is to get a good job (245). While finding a job and earning a decent living are certainly important elements of life, one's vocation or occupation represents just one element of the self. It also represents just one of many roles or responsibilities that humans are required to perform in life. Research strongly suggests that an individual's quality of life depends on attention to and development of all elements of the self. It's been found that people who attend to and integrate different dimensions of self, enabling them to live a well-rounded and well-balanced life, are more likely to be healthy (physically and mentally) and successful (personally and professionally) (78, 119, 139).

> "Wellness is an integrated method of functioning, which is oriented toward maximizing the potential of the individual."
>
> —H. Joseph Dunn, originator of the term "wellness"

Author's Experience—Joe Cuseo

On my bedroom door, I've posted a picture of the whole-person wheel (Figure 1. 4) to remind me to keep my life balanced. Every Sunday night I reflect on the previous week and ask myself if I've ignored any component of the holistic wheel. If I have, I try to make an earnest attempt to pay more attention to that aspect of my life during the upcoming week. For instance, if my previous week's activities reveal that I've neglected to spend enough time on my social self, I plan to spend more time the next week with family and friends. If I've neglected to attend to my physical self, I plan to exercise more consistently and eat more healthily the following week. Having the holistic wheel posted on my door provides me with a constant visual reminder to strive for "wholeness" and "balance" in my life.

The Co-Curriculum: Using the *Whole Campus* to Develop the *Whole Person*

> "The comprehensiveness of general education does not relate simply to knowledge, but to the entire environment in which learning takes place. From the beginning, general education curricula [the liberal arts] have been concerned with the student's total learning environment; the entire community is considered as a resource for general education."
>
> —George Miller, *The Meaning of General Education*

The power of the liberal arts is magnified when you take advantage of the total campus environment (261). A college education involves more than just taking courses and piling up credits; it also involves taking advantage of the learning opportunities available to you outside the classroom—known as the *co-curriculum*. Co-curricular experiences include all educational discussions you have with your peers and professors outside of class, as well as your participation in campus events, programs, and organizations sponsored by the Office of Student Life or Student Development.

Learning that takes place through the curriculum is primarily vicarious—that is, you learn from or through somebody else—by listening to professors in class and by reading outside of class. This type of academic learning is valuable, but it needs to be complemented by experiential learning—that is, learning that takes place directly from firsthand experiences. For example, leadership is not learned solely by listening to lectures and reading books about leadership. To fully develop your leadership skills, you need to have actual leadership experiences, such as "leading a [discussion] group in class, holding office in student government or by being captain of a sports team" (16).

Research has repeatedly shown that college students' out-of-class learning experiences contribute significantly to their personal development and professional success (171, 172, 232). This is one reason why most campuses no longer refer to them as "*extra*curricular" activities, but as *co*-curricular experiences—to send the message that they are equally important to learning and development as classroom-based experiences. For instance, students who engage in co-curricular leadership experiences in college make significant gains in measures of character development and civic engagement (30, 170). Students with co-curricular leadership experiences also report that these experiences equipped them with skills which enhanced their career performance and career advancement (19, 134). These alumni reports are confirmed by employers' job-performance evaluations, which indicate that co-curricular involvement during college—particularly if it involved leadership experience—is the best predictor of successful managerial performance (231, 232).

Author's Experience—Aaron Thompson

I strive to be a leader; I try to lead by example in both my personal and professional life. A truly effective leader must be able to adapt his or her style to the specific situation and people at hand. The best way to learn how to do this is by acquiring leadership experiences in multiple situations, both inside and outside the classroom.

I have found that effective leadership emerges from exposure to a variety of subject areas and ways of learning, including academic ("book learning") and experiential ("hands on" learning). My course work in the liberal arts and my leadership experiences in campus organizations taught me how to understand others, adapt my leadership style to their cultural background, and appreciate the multiple factors (e.g., personal, social, and global) that make positive change happen—which is what leadership is all about. The general education you acquire through the liberal arts curriculum, in conjunction with your co-curricular learning experiences outside the classroom, will combine to provide you with the broad perspectives and cross-situational skills needed to be a future leader.

KEY POINT

Capitalizing on experiential learning opportunities outside the classroom enables you to use your whole campus to develop yourself as a whole person.

Listed in **Box 1.2** are some of the major co-curricular programs and services offered on most college and university campuses; they are organized according to the primary dimension of the self they're designed to develop.

> "To educate liberally, learning experiences must be offered which facilitate maturity of the whole person. These are goals of student development and clearly they are consistent with the mission and goals of liberal education."
>
> —Theodore Berg, *Student Development and Liberal Education*

BOX 1.2

Dimensions of Holistic (Whole-Person) Development Promoted by Co-curricular Programs and Student Development Services

Intellectual Development
- Learning center
- College library
- Academic advising
- Tutoring services
- Information technology services
- Campus speakers
- Academic skills-development workshops
- Concerts, theater productions, and art shows

Ethical Development
- Judicial review board
- Student government
- Integrity committees and task forces

Physical Development
- Student health services
- Wellness programs
- Campus athletic activities and intramural sports

Spiritual Development
- Campus ministry
- Peer ministry
- Religious services

Vocational Development
- Career development services
- Internships programs
- Service learning experiences
- Work-study programs
- Major and career fairs

Personal Development
- Financial aid services and workshops
- Self-management workshops (e.g., managing time and money)
- Student development workshops and retreats

The list in Box 1.2 represents just a sample of the total number of out-of-class programs and services that may be available on your campus. As you can see from the list's length, colleges and universities are organized to promote student development in multiple ways. The power of the liberal arts is magnified when you combine coursework with co-curricular experiences and use the whole college to develop yourself as a whole person.

KEY POINT

A liberal arts education includes both the curriculum and the co-curriculum; they work together to produce college graduates who are both well rounded and globally minded.

PAUSE FOR THOUGHT

What student club or organization on your campus do you think can contribute most to your personal growth and development?

The Synoptic Perspective: Integrating the Multiple Perspectives of the Liberal Arts into a Coherent Whole

A liberal arts education not only involves taking multiple perspectives, but also integrating those perspectives into a meaningful whole (165, 223). Understanding how the perspectives of time, place, and person connect to create a unified whole is referred to as a *synoptic* perspective (80, 139). The word derives from a combination of two roots: *syn*—meaning "together" (as in the word "synthesize"), and *optic*—meaning "to see." Thus, a "synoptic" perspective literally means to "see things together" or "see the whole." Said in another way, it's a big-picture perspective that allows you to "connect the dots" and see how the trees form the forest.

"A truly great intellect is one which takes a connected view of old and new, past and present, far and near, and which has an insight into the influence of all these on one another, without which there is no whole, and no center."

—John Henry Newman, *The Idea of a University*

A synoptic perspective enables you to see how we, as individuals, fit into the larger scheme of things (88, 138). When we view ourselves as nested within a web of interconnections with other people, places, and times, we become aware of the common humanity we all share

> "Integration of learning is the ability to connect information from disparate contexts and perspectives—for example, to connect one field of study with another, the past with the present, one part with the whole—and vice versa."
>
> —Wabash National Study of Liberal Arts Education

(48). This increased sense of connection with humankind reduces our sense of personal isolation and alienation (29); it also increases our ability to empathize and identify with people whose life experiences differ radically from our own. In his book *The Perfect Education*, Kenneth Eble skillfully describes this benefit of a liberal arts education:

> It can provide that overarching life of a people, a community, a world that was going on before the individual came onto the scene and that will continue on after [s]he departs. By such means we come to see the world not alone. Our joys are more intense for being shared. Our sorrows are less destructive for our knowing universal sorrow. Our fears of death fade before the commonness of the occurrence (97).

KEY POINT

The liberal arts launch you on a quest for two forms of wholeness: (1) an *inner* wholeness in which key elements of self are connected to form the *whole person*, and (2) an *outer* wholeness in which you see yourself as connected to the *whole world*.

PAUSE FOR THOUGHT

What would you say is the key difference between acquiring *knowledge* versus learning a *skill*?

The Liberal Arts Develop Transferable Skills That Can Be Applied in Multiple Contexts

In addition to providing you with a broad base of knowledge and multiple perspectives for viewing yourself and the world around you, the liberal arts also equips you with a set of flexible skills that can be adapted for use in a wide variety of settings and contexts. This is another way in which the liberal arts are liberating—they supply you with a set of flexible skills that aren't tied to any particular subject area or career field—skills that can be transferred freely across different situations and contexts throughout life. These transferable skills are listed in the **Box 1.3**.

> **BOX 1.3**
>
> ### Transferable Lifelong-Learning Skills Developed by the Liberal Arts
>
> As you read the skills below, rate yourself on each of them, using the following scale:
> 4 = very strong, 3 = strong, 2 = needs some improvement, 1 = needs much improvement
>
> 1. **Critical and creative thinking**—ability to think innovatively and to evaluate the validity of ideas and arguments
> 2. **Communication**—ability to express and comprehend ideas through various media, which includes:
>   - **Written communication**—writing in a clear, creative, and persuasive manner
>   - **Oral communication**—speaking concisely, confidently, and eloquently
>   - **Reading**—comprehending, interpreting, and evaluating the literal and figurative meaning and connotations of words written in various styles and subjects
>   - **Listening**—comprehending spoken language actively, accurately, and empathically
>   - **Technological communication**—using electronic technology to effectively deliver and process ideas
> 3. **Quantitative skills**—ability to calculate, analyze, summarize, interpret, and evaluate quantitative information or statistical data
> 4. **Information literacy skills**—ability to access, retrieve, and evaluate information from various sources, including in-print and online (technology-based) systems

"Effectively managing personal affairs, from shopping for household products to selecting health care providers to making financial decisions, often requires people to acquire new knowledge from a variety of media, use different types of technologies and process complex information."

—The Partnership for 21st Century Skills

"Ability to recognize when information is needed and have the ability to locate, evaluate, and use it effectively."

—Definition of "information literacy," American Library Association Presidential Committee on Information Literacy

> "A liberal education is not something any of us ever achieve; it is not a state. Rather, it is a way of living... a way of educating ourselves without any illusion that our educations will ever be complete."
>
> —William Cronon, "Only Connect..." The Goals of a Liberal Education

A liberal arts education develops lifelong learning skills, such as the ability to access and retrieve information, which you can use to continually acquire new knowledge throughout life.

To use an athletic analogy, what the liberal arts do for the mind is similar to what cross-training does for the body. Cross-training engages the body in a wide range of exercises that promotes total physical fitness and develops a broad set of physical skills—strength, endurance, flexibility, and agility—which can be applied to improve performance in any sport or athletic endeavor. Similarly, the liberal arts engage the mind in a wide range of mental skills that can be used to improve performance in any major or career. As one scholar put it:

> Good learning habits can be transferred from one subject to another. When a basketball player lifts weights or plays handball in preparation for basketball, no one asks, "What good is weightlifting or handball for a basketball player?" because it is clear that these exercises build muscles, reflexes, and coordination that can be transferred to basketball—building them perhaps better than endless hours of basketball practice would. The same is true of the mind. Exercise in various areas builds brainpower for whatever endeavor you plan to pursue (133).

> "You know you've got to exercise your brain just like your muscles."
>
> —Will Rogers, Native American humorist and actor

Author's Experience—Joe Cuseo

I must confess that I graduated from college without ever truly understanding the true meaning and purpose of the liberal arts. When I became a college professor, two of my colleagues from the Office of Student Affairs asked me to help them create a first-year experience (college success) course. I agreed and volunteered to teach the course, which included a unit on the Meaning and Value of a Liberal Arts Education. When I researched the topic to prepare for class, I began to realize what the liberal arts were all about and what they did for me. It became clear that the lasting power of my college education didn't lie in all the factual information I studied in college (and forgotten), but in the transferable skills and "habits of mind" I took with me as a college graduate and have continued to use throughout my professional and personal life.

KEY POINT

A liberal arts education is not just "learning for its own sake." The skills developed by the liberal arts are also practical skills that can be transported and applied to improve personal and professional performance in "real life" throughout life. They are the mental "gift that keeps on giving."

Internet Resources

For additional information related to the ideas discussed in this chapter, see the following websites:
Understanding liberal education:
> www.aacu.org/resources/liberaleducation/index.cfm

"What is a liberal arts education?"
> www.iseek.org/education/liberalarts.html

Liberal Arts & Sciences online resources:
> www.educationindex.com/liberal

Chapter Summary and Highlights

The roots of the liberal arts date back to the origin of modern civilization—to the ancient Greeks and Romans who created a democratic republic in which citizens were given the freedom to elect their own leaders, thereby liberating them from uncritical dependence on an autocrat or dictator. Citizens of a democracy need to be skilled in the arts of critical thinking and persuasive communication in order to make wise choices about whom they elect as leaders and lawmakers, as well as to participate effectively in the democratic process. A liberal arts education was designed to supply them with these "skills for freedom." Thus, the original purpose of the liberal arts was not just career preparation; it was preparation for citizenship and leadership in a democratic nation. The liberal arts continue to be a distinctive feature of the American college and university system, differentiating it from other educational systems around the world.

Today, the liberal arts curriculum is sometimes referred to as *general education* to capture the fact that it supplies students with general knowledge and skills rather than narrow, specialized knowledge associated with a specific major or career. General education is what all college students learn, regardless of what their particular major or specialized field of study happens to be. It is the foundation of a college education on which all academic specializations (majors) are built; it represents what all college graduates should know and be able to do in order to succeed in any occupational path they choose to pursue. This is another way in which the liberal arts are liberating—they supply students with a set of flexible skills that aren't tied to any particular subject area or career field—skills that can be transferred freely across different situations and contexts throughout life.

The wide range of subjects that students encounter in the liberal arts also equips them with a wide-angle lens for viewing the world from a broader perspective—a "world view" that ensures their thinking is comprehensive and complete. This includes a social–spatial perspective that encompasses other people and places, and a chronological perspective on the past and its relationship to the present and future.

In addition to expanding our knowledge of the world around us, the liberal arts expand your knowledge of the world within you. Well-educated people not only look outward to learn about the world around them, they also look inward to learn about themselves. To "know thyself" is one of the most frequently cited goals of a liberal arts education. To know thyself—to be fully self-aware—requires knowledge of the *whole* self. The liberal arts liberate us from a narrow or single-dimensional view of ourselves, enabling us to become aware of and develop the multiple components of "self."

The power of the liberal arts is magnified when students take advantage of the total campus environment, which includes learning opportunities outside the classroom—known as the *co-curriculum*. Co-curricular experiences include out-of-class discussions with peers and professors, as well as participation in campus events, programs, and organizations sponsored by the Office of Student Life or Student Development. Capitalizing on experiential learning opportunities outside the classroom enables students to use the whole campus to develop themselves as whole persons.

In addition to developing awareness of the whole world and whole person, the liberal arts helps develop a *synoptic* perspective that views the individual as connected to and with the larger scheme of things. When we view ourselves as nested within a web of interconnections with other people, places, and times, we become aware of the common humanity we all share. Thus, the liberal arts launch us on a quest for two forms of wholeness: (1) an *inner* wholeness in which key elements of self are connected to form the *whole person*, and (2) an *outer* wholeness in which we see ourselves as connected to the *whole world*.

Questions and Final Reflections

1. Before you read this chapter, what did liberal arts or general education mean to you? After reading the chapter, in what ways (if any) has your understanding of the liberal arts or general education changed?

2. Identify the major disciplines (divisions of knowledge) listed in your campus catalog or bulletin. Write a short (one-paragraph) description that captures the distinctive educational goal or purpose of each discipline.

3. Review the mission and educational goals of your college or university.
   (a) In what ways do they align with, or differ from, the aims and purposes of the liberal arts?
   (b) What elements of the education mission or what educational goals of your campus matter most to you? Why?

4. To "broaden your horizons" and become a "well-rounded person" are commonly stated purposes of a college education. Describe specific ways in which the liberal arts do, in fact, broaden your horizons (perspectives) and promote your development as a well-rounded (whole) person.

5. In light of the ideas discussed in this chapter, how would you interpret or react to the following quotes?
    (a) "The aim of education is to enable individuals to continue their education. The object and reward of learning is continued capacity for growth."
    —John Dewey, American philosopher, psychologist, and educational reformer
    (b) "If you give a man a fish, you feed him for a day. If you teach a man how to fish, you feed him for life."
    —Author unknown
    (c) "The finest art, the most difficult art, is the art of living."
    —John Albert Macy, American author, poet, and editor of Helen Keller's autobiography

Benefits of the Liberal Arts

CHAPTER 2

PAUSE FOR THOUGHT

Before you begin reading this chapter, please answer the following question: Based on what you have read thus far in this book, what would you say is the major benefit of experiencing the liberal arts?

The purpose of this chapter is to pull together the major benefits of the liberal arts. Becoming aware of these benefits should increase your motivation to capitalize on them and articulate them. Employers and admissions directors of graduate and professional schools are more often interested in hearing about the outcomes of your college experience—the specific skills and attributes you developed in college, rather than the courses you took or the major you declared.

Ten research-based benefits (positive outcomes) of experiencing the liberal arts will be discussed in this chapter:

1. Broadening your personal interests and strengthening social self-confidence
2. Developing the capacity to learn more effectively and efficiently
3. Thinking critically from multiple perspectives
4. Thinking creatively
5. Exploring and selecting college majors and career options
6. Acquiring skills for success in your college major
7. Enhancing your career preparation and career success
8. Increasing your career options and occupational versatility
9. Strengthening your prospects for career advancement and leadership
10. Educating you for life

"Educated people can appreciate not only the front page of the *New York Times* but also the arts sections, the sports sections, the business section, the science section, and the editorials."

—William Cronon, *"Only Connect": The Goals of a Liberal Education*

"Only boring people get bored."

—Graffiti written in men's room at the main library, University of Iowa (circa 1977), author unknown

Broadening Your Personal Interests and Strengthening Social Self-Confidence

The breadth of knowledge and broad perspectives acquired through the liberal arts will expand your areas of personal interest and sources of mental stimulation. Studies show that people with a broad base of knowledge and a wide range of interests are less likely to experience boredom (124).

Your broader perspectives and wider range of knowledge will strengthen your social self-confidence. You'll be able to relate to a wider variety of people with a wider variety of educational, personal, and professional interests. Research indicates that as college students gain more general knowledge, they attain higher levels of self-esteem and social self-confidence (331, 232).

Developing the Capacity to Learn More Effectively and Efficiently

Learning takes place when the brain makes a physical (neurological) connection between what you're trying to learn and something you already know—that is, something that's already stored in your brain (see **Figure 2.1**). The greater the number and variety of connections you've stored in your brain, the easier it becomes for you to assimilate new information and connect it to what you already know (133, 294). In other words, broadening your base of knowledge creates a wider neurological net or web in which you can "catch" (connect) new ideas that you're trying to learn and retain. A liberal arts education increases the quantity and variety of neurological networks in your brain, thereby creating more pathways through which you can connect new ideas. You're more able to say when learning something new: "This reminds me of…" or "This relates to…," which (1) accelerates learning by facilitating the connection-making process and (2) strengthens learning by enabling the connections to become more deeply rooted. A broad base of knowl-

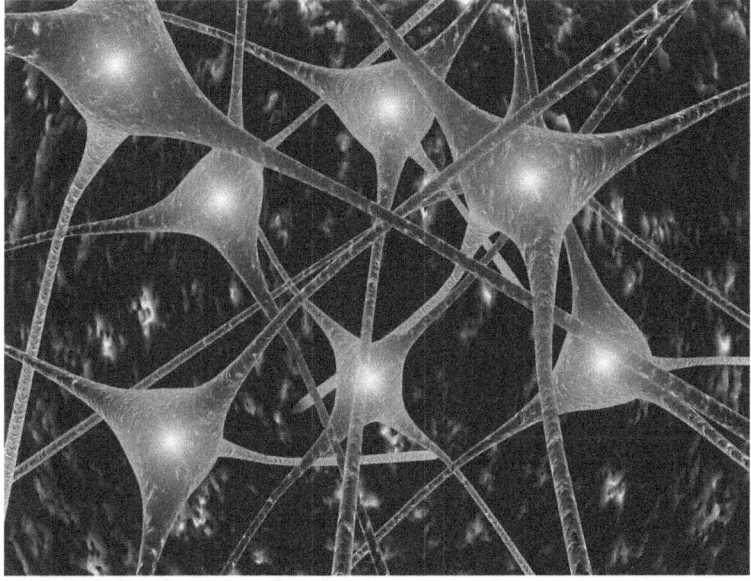

FIGURE 2.1 Learning derives from the Latin root *lira*, meaning "furrow" or "track." When we learn, a neurological track or path is created in our brain that connects what we are trying to learn to what we already know. When multiple and diverse connections have been made in the brain, the greater the number and variety of "hooks" become available to link (learn) new ideas. This enables subsequent learning to take place more rapidly and become more deeply rooted.

edge also helps you transfer knowledge to new situations; you're able to "decontextualize" it—detach it from the specific context in which it was originally learned and apply it in other contexts (16, 73).

Thinking Critically from Multiple Perspectives

> "To me, thinking at a higher level is when you approach a question or topic thoughtfully [and] you fully explore every aspect of that topic from all angles."
>
> —First-year college student

Important world issues, problems, and challenges do not come tightly packaged in separated academic disciplines or subject areas; instead, they present themselves in the context of an interconnected, multiple-perspective system. A good example of this multiperspective interconnectedness is the current issue of climate change. Addressing the issue of climate change requires a multidisciplinary perspective that includes:

* **Ecology**—understanding how humans interact with and preserve the natural environment
* **Physical Science**—researching and developing alternative sources of energy
* **Economics**—minimizing expenses incurred by industries for changing to different energy sources, or creating fiscal incentives for industries to make these changes
* **Political Science**—establishing laws that penalize industries for use of fossil-fuel-burning sources of energy
* **International Relations**—encouraging collaboration among different nations that are contributing to the current problem and could contribute to its eventual solution

Thus, a comprehensive understanding and solution to the global issue of climate change involves interrelationships among multiple perspectives (such as those summarized in **Box 2.1**), each of which is developed by the liberal arts.

Effective decision making and problem solving requires what scholars call "systems thinking"—understanding how our actions affect and are affected by other parts of a larger, interconnected system. "Systems thinking is a discipline for seeing whole. It is

Humanity, Diversity, and the Liberal Arts: Foundation of a College Education

BOX 2.1

Taking Multiple Perspectives: Implications for the Issue of Climate Change

Perspective	Implication
Person	Climate change involves humans at a personal level because individual efforts to conserve energy in our homes and our willingness to purchase energy-efficient products can play a significant role in addressing this problem.
Place	Climate change is an international phenomenon that extends beyond the boundaries of any one country and requires the joint effort of different nations around the world.
Time	If the current trend toward higher global temperatures continues, it could seriously threaten the lives of future generations of people inhabiting the planet.

a framework for seeing interrelationships rather than things, for seeing patterns of change rather than static 'snapshots.' And systems thinking is a sensibility—for the subtle interconnectedness that gives living systems their unique character" (256). The concept of systems thinking underscores the importance of viewing issues from multiple perspectives, such as those developed by the liberal arts.

PAUSE FOR THOUGHT

> Think of a current national or international problem (other than climate change) whose solution requires multiple perspective-taking or systems thinking.

> "I would go to the library and borrow scores by all those great composers, like Stravinsky, Alban Berg, Prokofiev. I wanted to see what was going on in all of music."
>
> —Miles Davis, highly influential twentieth-century musician who contributed to such innovative forms of jazz music as hard bop, cool jazz, free jazz, and fusion

Thinking Creatively

Creativity typically emerges from a broad base of knowledge, perspectives, and skill sets that extend beyond the boundaries of a single, specialized field of study (157). Studies of creative people reveal they have a wide range of interests and knowledge that typically crosses disciplinary boundaries, which enables them to draw on ideas from multiple subject areas (21, 249). Experiencing the variety of disciplines and perspectives developed by the liberal arts serves to stimulate creativity by enabling you to develop different thinking styles and strategies that can be mixed and matched to generate innovative ideas.

> "Liberally educated people have been liberated by their education to explore and fulfill the promise of their own highest talents."
>
> —William Cronon, *"Only Connect..." The Goals of a Liberal Education*

Exploring and Selecting College Majors and Career Options

Self-awareness is the critical first step toward making effective personal decisions and life choices. You need to know yourself well before you can know what major or career is best for you. The breadth and depth of questions you're exposed to in the liberal arts will help you become more deeply aware of different dimensions of yourself, including those that are critical for making effective decisions about majors and careers, namely:

Humanity, Diversity, and the Liberal Arts: Foundation of a College Education

- **Interests**—what you *like* to do
- **Talents**—what you have the ability to do *well*
- **Values**—what you believe is *important* to do and is really *worth* doing

The opportunity to make a reasonable amount of money is certainly one factor to consider when choosing a career, but deciding on a college major and eventual career path should involve factors other than your expected starting salary. This decision should also involve deep awareness and strong consideration of your special abilities, what you're passionate about, and what fulfills you. Remember that the word *vocation* derives from the Latin *vocatio,* meaning "a calling," which suggests that your line of work should call forth your true talents, interests, and values.

Research on students' decision-making patterns about a college major reveal that:

- less than 10 percent of new college students feel they know a great deal about the field that they intend to major in;
- as students proceed through the first year of college, they grow more uncertain about the major they chose when they began college;
- more than two-thirds of new students change their mind about their major during the first year of college; and
- only one in three college seniors graduate in the same field that they chose during their first year of college (87).

These findings demonstrate that the vast majority of students entering college are uncertain about their academic specialization and career direction. Most college students don't reach a final decision about their major *before* starting college; typically, they make that decision *during* their college experience.

Being initially undecided about a major is nothing that college students should be embarrassed about; in fact, they may be undecided for very good reasons. New students may be undecided simply because they have interests in multiple subjects. This is a healthy form of indecision indicating they have a wide range of interests and a

> "In order to succeed, you must know what you are doing, like what you are doing, and believe in what you are doing."
>
> —Will Rogers, American actor and humorist

> "Know thyself and to thine own self be true."
>
> —Polonius in *Hamlet*, a play by William Shakespeare

> "All who wander are not lost."
>
> —J. R. R. Tolkien, *Lord of the Rings*

> "The best words of wisdom that I could give new freshmen [are] not to feel like you need to know what you want to major in right away. They should really use their first two years to explore all of the different classes available. They may find a hidden interest in something they never would have considered. I know this from personal experience."
>
> —Advice to new students from a college sophomore (291)

high level of intellectual curiosity. Students may also be undecided because they are reflective, deliberate thinkers who prefer to explore their options carefully before making a firm and final commitment. This is supported by a national study of students who were undecided about a major at the start of college which revealed that 43 percent had several ideas in mind but were not yet ready to commit to one of them (121).

To be at least somewhat uncertain about educational goals during the early stages of the college experience is only natural because students have yet to experience the variety of subjects and academic programs that comprise the college curriculum. In fact, one purpose of general education is to help new students develop the critical thinking skills needed to make wise choices and well-informed decisions, including choices and decisions about a college major. The liberal arts curriculum introduces students to new fields of study, some of which they've never experienced before. As students progress through this curriculum, they may discover new subjects that capture their interest, uncover their hidden talents, and find options for college majors that "fit" them well.

A key benefit of experiencing the variety of courses that make up the liberal arts curriculum is that they enable you to become more aware of yourself and, at the same time, become more aware of the variety of academic disciplines and subject areas that are available to you as potential majors. As you gain experience with the college curriculum, you gain greater insight into your academic interests, strengths, and weaknesses. This is important self-knowledge to take into consideration when choosing a major because you want to pursue a field that capitalizes on your intellectual curiosity, abilities, and talents. Look at your excursion through the liberal arts curriculum as an exploratory journey during which you should be armed and ready to make three key discoveries:
1. Discovering the full range of choices for majors available to you
2. Discovering where your special interests, talents, and values lie
3. Discovering what specialized field of study provides the best "fit" for your personal interests, talents, and values

Author's Experience—Aaron Thompson

I took Introduction to Sociology and Marriage and Family in college just to fulfill general education requirements. Unexpectedly, both courses ended up having a much larger, long-term effect on my educational and professional development. Sociology proved so interesting to me that it became my major and I went on to earn a Ph.D. in the field. The Marriage and Family course intrigued me so much that I went on to conduct research and write two books on the topic. Looking back, I would have never expected that those two courses, which I took just to fulfill general education requirements, would have such a significant impact on my future. Moral of this story: When you're taking liberal arts courses, you can do more than just fulfill general education requirements. If you keep an open mind and are willing to learn, the liberal arts can have a profound and productive impact on your choice of a college major and your eventual career path.

Acquiring Skills for Success in Your College Major

General education shouldn't be viewed as something unrelated or irrelevant to your major; the liberal arts represent the component of the college experience that provides the overall context and underlying skills needed for success in any specialized field of study. Recall our story at the very start of this book about Laura, the student with a business major who questioned why she had to take a course in philosophy. Laura's philosophy course not only fulfilled a general education requirement, it also developed critical thinking and ethical reasoning skills that she could apply to delve into business issues more deeply and respond to them more humanely. It also enabled her to gain understanding of important philosophical issues embedded in business practice, such as (1) the underlying assumptions and values of capitalism relative to other economic systems (e.g., socialism and economic systems that blend socialistic and capitalistic elements), (2) business ethics (e.g., fair hiring and firing practices), and (3) business justice (e.g., fair and equitable distribution of profits shared among workers, executives, and shareholders).

"A general education supplies a context for all knowledge and especially for one's chosen area. Every field gives only a partial view of knowledge and an exclusive or overemphasis on one field of study distorts the understanding of reality."

—Robert Harris, *On the Purpose of a Liberal Arts Education*

Similarly, other subjects in the liberal arts curriculum provide business majors (and the many non-business majors who end up working in business organizations) with essential knowledge and deep thinking skills needed to succeed in the corporate world, such as:

- **History and Political Science**—understanding governmental policies that impact business operations and regulations
- **Psychology and Sociology**—understanding how human motives and human choices, both individually and collectively, affect the productivity of workers and consumer purchasing habits
- **Speech, English Composition, and Literature**—speaking confidently and persuasively at corporate meetings, writing clear and concise memos, reading and interpreting business reports accurately and critically
- **Mathematics**—analyzing and interpreting statistical data from marketing surveys
- **Natural Science**—determining effective and efficient ways for companies to conserve energy and sustain natural resources
- **Fine Arts**—designing visually engaging advertisements and marketing strategies
- **Physical and Health Education**—selecting effective employee health-insurance plans and corporate-sponsored health services

> "Virtually all occupational endeavors require a working appreciation of the historical, cultural, ethical, and global environments that surround the application of skilled work."
>
> —Robert Jones, author, *Liberal Education for the Twenty-first Century: Business Expectations*

These same liberal arts subjects are relevant to successful performance in fields other than business. For instance, successful performance in all majors and professions requires a historical perspective and ethical perspective because all of them have a history and none of them are value-free.

In his classic work, *The Idea of a University*, John Henry Newman eloquently explains how a liberal arts education prepares students for any major or career:

> It is the education which gives a man [woman] a clear conscious view of his own opinions and judgments, a truth in developing them, an eloquence in expressing them, and a force in urging them. It teaches him to see things as they are, to go right to the point, to detect what is sophisticated, and to

discard what is irrelevant. It prepares him to fill any post with credit, and to master any subject with facility (217).

Although you may specialize in a particular field of study, real-life issues and challenges aren't conveniently divided into specialized majors. Important and enduring issues—such as finding meaning and purpose in life, providing effective leadership, combating prejudice, and reducing international conflict—can neither be fully understood nor effectively solved with the thinking tools of a single academic discipline. Approaching important, multifaceted issues from the perspective of a single, specialized field of study would be akin to applying a simple, one-dimensional tool to a complex, multidimensional problem.

Author's Experience—Joe Cuseo

When I decided on my major (psychology), I thought that the best thing I could do to succeed in my chosen field was to take as many psychology courses as possible. Whenever I had room in my schedule for a free elective, I would use it to take another psychology course. Looking back, I realize this was a poor decision. After beginning my career as a professor of psychology, I soon discovered that a deep and complete understanding of the human mind and human behavior (two key goals of my profession) requires a broad base of knowledge that goes well beyond the boundaries of the field of psychology. It involves knowledge of (1) philosophy—how the methods used by psychology to study human behavior derive from and rest on certain philosophical positions or assumptions, (2) biology—how brain chemistry affects human feelings and emotions, (3) sociology—how group behavior and societal norms affect individual behavior, and (4) history—how major events in the world that take place at the time individuals are growing up can influence their attitudes, beliefs, and fears.

Don't make the same mistake I did. Use at least some of your college electives to broaden your scope of knowledge and to learn about things you know little or nothing about. This will do more than make you a more "well rounded" or well-educated person; it will also pay practical dividends by improving your performance in your college major and future career.

"The psychologist who would fully understand the variety of mental problems his patients may suffer will need a wide-ranging knowledge to recognize that some problems are biological, some are spiritual, some are the products of environment. If he [she] never studies biology, theology, or sociology, how will he be able to treat his patients well?"

—Robert Harris, *On the Purpose of a Liberal Arts Education*

PAUSE FOR THOUGHT

What three skills or attributes do you think are most important for career success in today's work world?

Enhancing Your Career Preparation and Career Success

The world has changed dramatically in the twenty-first century, and the world of work has changed with it. What are today's employers looking for in the people they hire? They are seeking workers who can problem-solve and manage projects; they want employees with effective interpersonal skills who can work well with groups; they also want their new hires to be skilled communicators who are able to adapt to a variety of environments.

> "From Utah to the Ukraine and from Milwaukee to Manila, industry is demanding that our graduates have better teamwork skills, communication abilities, and an understanding of the socioeconomic context in which engineering is practiced."
>
> —Ernest Smerdon, president of the American Society for Engineering Education

In particular, employers believe that the following skills and perspectives should be key outcomes of a college education that will leave graduates well prepared for work in the twenty-first century (18).

- Integrative learning:
   o Ability to apply knowledge and skills to real-world settings
- Knowledge of human cultures, the physical world, and the natural world, which includes understanding of:
   o Concepts and new developments in science and technology
   o Global issues and developments and their implications for the future
   o The role of the United States in the world
   o Cultural values and traditions in America and other countries

Humanity, Diversity, and the Liberal Arts: Foundation of a College Education

- Intellectual and practical skills:
  - Ability to effectively communicate orally and in writing
  - Critical thinking and analytical reasoning skills
  - Ability to locate, organize, and evaluate information from multiple sources
  - Ability to be innovative and think creatively
  - Ability to solve complex problems
  - Ability to work with numbers and understand statistics
- Personal and social responsibility:
  - Teamwork skills and the ability to collaborate with others in diverse group settings
  - A sense of integrity and ethics

The foregoing skills and qualities are best developed by a well-rounded education that combines general education through the liberal arts and specialized education in a specific major. Interviews with hundreds of recent college graduates and employers indicate that both groups believe the best preparation for career entry is a college education that provides career-specific preparation plus broad-based knowledge and flexible skills (134,136). In fact, 93 percent of employers agree that a candidate's capacity to think critically, communicate clearly, and solve complex problems is more important than his or her undergraduate major (136).

If you were to synthesize all the findings from national surveys and personal interviews with employers and executives about the type of skills they seek in college graduates, you would find that they fall consistently into the following three categories.

1. **Communication skills**—listening, speaking, writing, and reading (60, 61, 134)
   According to Marilyn Mackes, Executive Director of the National Association of Colleges and Employers, "There is such a heavy emphasis on effective communication in the workplace that college students who master these skills can set themselves apart from the pack when searching for employment" (185).
2. **Thinking skills**—critical thinking, creative thinking, and problem solving (65, 106, 60, 134, 98)

> "The members of my senior team all graduated with a liberal arts degree, from history to political science, music to sociology. What makes them a strong team is they come from different backgrounds and are all flexible, dynamic thinkers."
>
> —Alan Buckelew, CEO of Princess Cruises (288)

> "They asked me during my interview why I was right for the job and I told them because I can read well, write well, and I can think. They really liked that because those were the skills they were looking for."
>
> —English major hired by a public relations firm (182)

CHAPTER 2: Benefits of the Liberal Arts

> "At State Farm, our [employment] exam does not test applicants on their knowledge of finance or the insurance business, but it does require them to demonstrate critical thinking skills and the ability to calculate and think logically. These skills plus the ability to read for information, to communicate and write effectively need to be demonstrated."
>
> —Edward B. Rust Jr., chairman and CEO, State Farm Insurance Companies (18)

National surveys indicate that 95 percent of employers give hiring preference to college graduates with skills that will enable them to contribute to innovation in the workplace (136). According to Paul Dominski, store recruiter for the Robinson-May Department Stores Company, "We look for people who can think critically and analytically. If you can do those things, we can teach you our business" (146).

3. **Lifelong learning skills**—ability and willingness to learn continually throughout life (61, 272)

    Over 90 percent of employers report that the capacity for ongoing professional development and continued learning is important. Over 6 percent report that it is very important (136).

The current global economy has progressed from being agrarian (farm-based) to industrial (machine-based) to technological (information-based). The technological revolution is generating information and new knowledge at a faster rate than at any other time in human history (95). When knowledge is produced and communicated at such rapid rates, existing knowledge quickly becomes obsolete (204). In order to perform their jobs and advance in their careers, workers in today's complex, fast-changing world must continually update their skills and learn new skills (220). This need for lifelong learning creates demand for workers who have *learned how to learn* and how to continue learning throughout life. This is a hallmark of the liberal arts and a key attribute of successful college graduates. (It's also the reason why college graduation is referred to as *commencement*—a beginning, not an end.)

> "The only person who is educated is the one who has learned how to learn and change."
>
> —Carl Rogers, influential humanistic psychologist and Nobel Peace Prize nominee

PAUSE FOR THOUGHT

Among the three key skills emphasized by today's employers (communication, higher-level thinking, and lifelong learning), which one of them did you least expect to be on the list? Why?

The remarkable resemblance between the work skills sought by current employers and the lifelong learning skills developed by the liberal arts is not surprising when you think about the typical duties and responsibilities of working professionals. They need good communication skills to listen, speak, describe, and explain ideas to co-workers and customers. They need advanced reading skills to critically interpret and evaluate written material; they need quantitative reasoning skills to analyze statistical data; and they need writing skills to compose numerous memos, letters, and reports. They must also possess an assortment of higher-level thinking skills in order to analyze problems, construct well-organized plans, generate creative ideas and problem solutions, and critically assess whether their plans and strategies are working effectively.

KEY POINT

The sharp distinction often drawn between the "liberal arts" and "pre-professional" fields is a false dichotomy—an artificial divide. A liberal arts education is not just "learning for its own sake"; it also develops practical skills that contribute to successful long-term performance in any career. Said in another way: General education *is* career preparation.

While communication skills, higher-level thinking, and lifelong learning consistently rank high in importance to employers, they do not constitute the complete list of skills they seek in college graduates. Employers also place high value on the following three sets of personal characteristics.

"In times of change, learners inherit the earth . . . [they] find themselves beautifully equipped to deal with a world that no longer exists."

—Eric Hoffer, author of *The Ordeal of Change* and recipient of the Presidential Medal of Freedom

1. **Interpersonal (social) intelligence**—leadership skills, ability to collaborate, negotiate, work in teams, and relate to others with diverse characteristics and cultural backgrounds (32, 111, 129)
2. **Personal qualities and behaviors**—initiative, motivation, self-management, independence, personal responsibility, enthusiasm, flexibility, and self-esteem (60, 206, 134)
3. **Personal ethics**—honesty, integrity, and ethical standards of conduct (111). In a recent national survey of employers,

CHAPTER 2: Benefits of the Liberal Arts

> "360-degree type people. That's exactly what we're looking for. Sometimes we get very technical people who are able to manage budgets and do the technical work, but their social skills just aren't very good."
>
> —Fairfax Business Executive (134)

96 percent rated "ethical judgment and integrity" as an important outcome of a college education; 76 percent rated it as very important (136).

Notice that the personal attributes sought by employers correspond closely to the elements of the "whole person" developed through general education (the curriculum and co-curriculum). Also note that many of these employer-sought attributes (e.g., personal initiative, self-management, and personal responsibility) are consistent with the liberal arts' goal of liberating students to become independent thinking, self-directed human beings.

Author's Experience—Aaron Thompson

> "I look for people that take responsibility and are good team people over anything else. I can teach [them] the technical."
>
> —Milwaukee Business Executive (134)

After graduating from college, I spent the first ten years of my professional life working in corporate America. I held management and leadership roles during most of those years. As part of my job, I had the responsibility of hiring new employees and identifying the skills that most often were associated with success at the company. I identified four key skill sets and had them at the top of my list whenever I assessed new employees: (1) writing—ability to express ideas in print; (2) interpersonal skills—ability to get along well with others; (3) negotiation skills—ability to resolve conflict and bring about agreement with others; and (4) problem-solving skills—ability to identify the source of a problem and generate solutions.

If a job candidate did not have these skills, he or she could not move on to the next level of the selection process, which involved discussion of specific knowledge and technical skills relating to the position. As you can see, the four core skills at the top of my list were among the core skills developed by general education.

Increasing Your Career Options and Occupational Versatility

Another way in which the liberal arts "liberate" you is by freeing you from narrow specialization; they increase your career options by equipping you with flexible work skills that are applicable to a wide range of work tasks and professional positions. These transferable skills contribute to your vocational freedom in three major ways: (1) they increase initial options for career *entry*—your ability to enter different types of careers immediately after college, (2) they increase career *mobility*—your ability to move from one career to another throughout the course of your career, and (3) they increase opportunities for career *reentry*—your ability to move back into a career path after leaving it temporarily (e.g., to care for young children).

Interviews with newly hired college graduates indicate only about 50 percent of them expect to continue working in the same field in which they are currently employed. (134) Follow-up studies on college graduates at later stages in their career reveal that they already have changed careers at least once, and the further along they are in their career path, the more likely they are to be working in a field unrelated to their college major. (18) This may seem surprising, but keep in mind that the liberal arts represent a significant portion of a college education; it is this component of a college education that equips students with breadth of knowledge and transferable skills (e.g., writing, speaking, thinking, information literacy) that enable them to perform well in a variety of careers, regardless of what their particular college major happened to be.

In today's economy, which is being fueled by rapid advances in technology and an explosion of new knowledge, career versatility becomes especially important. During periods of rapid change, existing jobs can become quickly outdated and obsolete (196); at the same time, entirely new positions emerge that never existed before (53). Nobody can receive specialized training or preparation to fill these unanticipated positions because no one knows exactly what specific knowledge and skills will be required by the position. This creates high demand for *generalists* who possess a broad base of knowledge, flexible life-

> "Everybody ten years out of college is probably doing something completely different than what they majored in. I got a degree in electrical engineering. Right off the bat I started in software and I moved into sales and then into management; the well-rounded portion of what I got in college is what really served me."
>
> —Business executive (134)

> "The fixed person for the fixed duties, who in older societies was a blessing, in the future will be a public danger."
>
> —Alfred North Whitehead, English mathematician and philosopher

long-learning skills, and the mental versatility needed to accommodate new work roles and changing professional responsibilities (220). Employers report that their companies and organizations are now asking employees to take on greater responsibilities that require a broader set of skills (135). According to a national survey of employers, new employees are expected to engage in the following tasks more frequently today than in the past:

- Work harder to coordinate with other departments
- Address challenges that are more complex
- Use higher levels of thinking and a wider range of knowledge (136)

Author's Experience—Joe Cuseo

My father is a good example of someone whose education was too narrow and whose career was too specialized. He spent approximately two years of his life learning to be a horologist—a specialist in watch and clock repair. He found regular employment for over thirty years of his working life, but advances in technology made it possible for companies to produce and sell high-performance watches at much cheaper prices than ever before. As a result, when their watches began to wear out or malfunction, people didn't pay to have them repaired; they simply threw them away and bought new ones. This reduced society's need for watch repairmen, such as my father, who soon lost his position with the watch company he was working for and was forced into early retirement.

> "It is far more important for students to develop transferable skills and capacities than to choose a 'hot' major in a field that will quickly either 'cool' or be replaced by other priority fields."
>
> —Debra Humphreys, vice president for communications and public affairs, Association of American Colleges and Universities

While specific technological skills and positions may be "hot" right now, the demand for narrow skills tied to specific technologies, such as those relating to current computer software and Web page designs, are likely to change considerably in the near future. Highly specialized technical skills tend to be seasonal—they come and go with passage of time (like the "flavor of the month"). Currently, they may be on the "cutting edge" but that edge will soon get frayed and be replaced with newer, sharper-edged technology. In contrast, transferable, lifelong-learning skills that are needed to develop and apply new technological tools—such as thinking creatively and critically, solving problems effectively, and communicating with clarity—are perennial; they will continue to remain in demand because their relevance is timeless. The transferable skills developed by the liberal arts may not be "edgy," but they're stable, durable, and applicable to every new wave of technological change.

KEY POINT

While the need for specialized, technical skills will continue to fluctuate with changes in the nature of technology, the liberal arts equip you with lifelong-learning skills and perspectives that are neither trendy nor time-bound. The best way to prepare for today's world of work is to develop skills that are timeless and flexible. This is exactly what the liberal arts are designed to do.

PAUSE FOR THOUGHT

Compared to being initially hired, what skills or attributes do you think are more important for career *promotion* and *advancement*?

Strengthening Your Prospects for Career Advancement and Leadership

Studies show that as the careers of college graduates progress, the narrower skills learned in their specialized major tend to decline in importance and are replaced by more general skills (232). Specialized skills provide you with *initial* job readiness, and in some careers, these specialized skills can be learned early through on-the-job training. Broad-based knowledge and general skills, such as thinking and communicating, become more critical as you move up the career ladder. They also reduce your risk of being promoted to a position that you cannot perform successfully because it requires a broader set of skills

"As times goes on, the technical and practical skills that vocational majors learn in college become less important to continued success. Such abilities as communication skills, human relations, creativity, and 'big picture thinking' matter more."

—Derek Bok,
President Emeritus,
Harvard University

> "A solid foundation in the liberal arts and sciences is necessary for those who want to be corporate leaders."
>
> —George C. Nolen, president and CEO, Siemens Corporation, New York (18)

than were needed in lower-level positions. This scenario is sometimes referred to as the "Peter Principle"—employees getting promoted to a more advanced position based on their successful performance in a lower-level position, but then performing poorly in the higher-level position because they lack the higher-level skills it requires (237).

As the twenty-first century unfolds, the demand for higher-level management and leadership positions is expected to exceed the supply of workers available to fill these positions. (140) In a recent national survey, the majority of employers report that college graduates have the skills and knowledge to succeed in entry-level positions, but only 44 percent believe that graduates will have the skills required for success at higher-level positions (136). What will be needed to perform well in these higher-level positions is the broad-based knowledge and transferable skills developed by the liberal arts.

KEY POINT

A successful career is not a short sprint but a long-distance race that will unfold over an extended period of time. The liberal arts provide you with sustainable skills that serve you over the long haul. Don't underestimate the long-lasting value of these skills; they will open doors for career advancement throughout your working life.

> "The only education that prepares us for change is a liberal education. In periods of change, narrow specialization condemns us to inflexibility—precisely what we do not need. We need the flexible intellectual skills to be problem solvers, to be able to continue learning over time."
>
> —David Kearns, former CEO of Xerox Corporation

Educating You for Life

Studies show that students often view general education as something to "get out of the way" or "get behind them" (18). Don't buy into the belief that general education courses represent a series of hoops and hurdles that must be surmounted or circumnavigated before you get to do what really matters. Instead of viewing them as courses to get "out of the way," get "into them" and keep in mind you'll take away from them a set of skills with two powerful qualities:

1. **Flexibility: skills that are *portable*—**They "travel well"; you can carry them with you and apply them across a wide range of work situations and life roles.

2. **Durability: skills that are *sustainable*** — They have long-lasting value; you can continue to use them across changing times and different stages of life.

> **KEY POINT**
>
> You're likely to forget much of the specialized, factual information learned in college. However, you will retain the ways of thinking, habits of mind, and communication skills developed by the liberal arts, and you will continue to use them in multiple life roles throughout life.

Author's Experience—Joe Cuseo

One life role that a liberal arts education helped prepare me to perform was that of a parent. Courses I took in psychology and sociology proved to be useful in helping me understand my son's development and how I could best support him at different stages of his life. Surprisingly, there was one course I had in college that I never expected would help me as a parent, but it eventually did. That course was statistics, which I took merely to fulfill a general education requirement in mathematics. It was not a particularly enjoyable course; in fact, some of my classmates sarcastically referred to it as "sadistics" because they felt it was a torturous and painful experience. However, what I learned in that course became very valuable to me many years later when my 14-year-old son (Tony) developed a life-threatening disease known as leukemia—a form of cancer that attacks blood cells. Tony had a particularly perilous form of leukemia that had only a 35 percent survival rate; almost two of every three patients who developed the disease died within seven years. This statistic was based on patients receiving the traditional treatment of chemotherapy, which was the type of treatment that my son began receiving when his cancer was first detected.

Another option for treating Tony's cancer was a bone-marrow transplant, which involved using radiation to destroy all of his own bone marrow (that was making the abnormal blood cells) and replacing it with bone marrow donated to him by another person. My wife and I got opinions from doctors at two major cancer centers—one from a center that specialized in chemotherapy, and one from a center that specialized in bone-marrow transplants.

The chemotherapy doctors felt strongly that drug treatment would be the better way to treat and cure my son; however, the bone-marrow transplant doctors felt just as strongly that his chances of survival would be much better if he had a transplant. Thus, my wife and I had to decide between two opposing recommendations, each made by a respected group of doctors.

To help us reach a decision, I asked both teams of doctors for research studies on the effectiveness of chemotherapy and bone-marrow transplants for treating my son's particular type of cancer. I read all these studies and carefully reviewed their statistical findings. I remembered from my statistics course that when an average is calculated for a general group of people (e.g., average cure rate for people with leukemia) it tends to lump together individuals from different subgroups (e.g., males and females; children, teenagers, and adults). Sometimes, an average statistic calculated for a whole group tends to mask or camouflage differences among different subgroups that make up the whole group. So, when I read the research reports, I dug deeper to find any subgroup statistics that were embedded in the reports. I found two subgroups of patients with my son's particular type of cancer that had a higher rate of cure with chemotherapy than the general (whole-group) average of 35 percent. One subgroup included people with a low number of abnormal cells at the time their cancer was first diagnosed, and the other subgroup consisted of people whose cancer cells dropped rapidly after their first week of chemotherapy. My son belonged to both of these subgroups, which meant that his chance for cure with chemotherapy was higher than the overall 35 percent average. Furthermore, I found that the statistics for successful bone-marrow transplants were based only on patients whose body accepted the donor's bone marrow; they did not include patients who died because their body initially rejected it. Thus, the success rate for bone-marrow patients was not as high it appeared to be, because the overall average didn't include the subgroup of patients who died as result of transplant rejection rather than the cancer itself. Based on these statistics, I decided to have my son undergo chemotherapy rather than the bone-marrow transplant.

My son has now been cancer free for almost 10 years, so it looks like I made the right decision. I never imagined, however, that a statistics course, which I took many years ago to fulfill a general education requirement, would help me fulfill my role as a parent and help me make a life-or-death decision about my only son.

KEY POINT

A liberal arts education not only prepares you for a career; it prepares you for life.

BOX 2.2

Tying It Altogether: The Wide-Ranging and Long-Lasting Benefits of a College Education

When college graduates are compared with people from similar social and economic backgrounds who did not continue their education beyond high school, research reveals that a college education is well worth it—in terms of both personal development and career advancement. Graduating from college brings with it a variety of long-term benefits, which are listed below. Note that they are wide-ranging, affecting development of the whole individual and society at large. These broad-based benefits serve as testimony to the power of the liberal arts component of a college education.

1. **Career Benefits**
    - **Career security and stability**—lower rate of unemployment and lower risk of being laid off work
    - **Career versatility and mobility**—greater ability to move from one position to another
    - **Career advancement**—more opportunity to move up to higher-level professional positions
    - **Career interest**—more likely to work in positions they find stimulating and challenging
    - **Career satisfaction**—more likely to find their work fulfilling and feel that it allows them to use their special talents
    - **Career autonomy**—greater independence and opportunity to make their own decisions
    - **Career prestige**—more likely to hold higher-status positions, that is, jobs considered to be desirable and highly regarded by society

"For the individual, having access to and successfully graduating from an institution of higher education has proved to be the path to a better job, to better health and to a better life."

—College Board (71)

> "An investment in knowledge always pays the best interest."
>
> —Ben Franklin, scientist, inventor, and a founding father of the United States

2. **Economic Advantages**
   - Make more effective consumer choices and decisions
   - Make wiser long-term investments
   - Receive greater pension benefits
   - Earn higher income: The gap between the earnings of high school and college graduates is *growing*. Individuals holding a bachelor's degree now earn an average annual salary of over $65,000 per year—40 percent higher than high school graduates—whose average salary is less than $38,000 per year. When these differences are calculated over a lifetime, the income of families headed by people with a bachelor's degree is over $1 million more than families headed by people with a high school diploma.

3. **Advanced Intellectual Skills**
   - Greater knowledge
   - More effective problem-solving skills
   - Better ability to deal with complex and ambiguous (uncertain) problems
   - Greater openness to new ideas
   - More advanced levels of moral reasoning
   - Clearer sense of self-identity—greater awareness and knowledge of personal talents, interests, values, and needs
   - Greater likelihood of learning continually throughout life

4. **Better Physical Health**
   - Better health insurance—more more likely to be covered and more comprehensive coverage
   - Better dietary habits
   - Exercise more regularly
   - Have lower rates of obesity
   - Live longer and healthier lives

5. **Social Benefits**
   - Greater social self-confidence
   - Better ability to understand and communicate effectively with others

> "Without exception, the observed changes [during college] involve greater breadth, expansion, and appreciation for the new and different. These changes are eminently consistent with values of a liberal [arts] education, and the evidence for their presence is compelling."
>
> —Ernest Pascarella and Pat Terenzini, *How College Affects Students*

- Greater popularity
- More effective leadership skills
- Higher levels of marital satisfaction

6. **Emotional Benefits**
    - Lower levels of anxiety
    - Higher levels of self-esteem
    - Greater sense of self-efficacy—believe they have more influence and control over their lives
    - Higher levels of psychological well-being
    - Higher levels of life satisfaction and happiness

7. **Effective Citizenship**
    - Greater interest in national issues—both social and political
    - Greater knowledge of current affairs
    - Higher voting participation rates
    - Higher rates of participation in civic affairs and community service

8. **Higher Quality of Life for Their Children**
    - Less likely to smoke during pregnancy
    - Provide better health care for their children
    - Spend more time with their children
    - More likely to involve their children in educational activities that stimulate their mental development
    - More likely to save money for their children to go to college
    - More likely to have children who graduate from college
    - More likely that their children will attain higher-status, higher-salary careers

> "My three-month-old boy is very important to me, and it is important I graduate from college so my son, as well as I, live a better life"
>
> —First-year student's response to the question: "What is most important to you?"

Sources: 13, 19, 44, 45, 71, 72, 91, 104, 129, 130, 232, 255, 276, 283

PAUSE FOR THOUGHT

Glance back at the eight benefits or positive outcomes of a college education listed in **Box 2.2**. If you were to rank them in terms of their importance to you, which three would rank at the top your list? Why?

Internet Resources

For additional information related to the ideas discussed in this chapter, see the following websites:

21st Century Skills: http://edglossary.org/21st-century-skills/

"The value of a liberal arts education in today's global marketplace." http://www.huffingtonpost.com/edward-j-ray/the-value-of-a-liberal-arts-education_b_3647765.html

"Liberal arts grads win long-term." https://www.insidehighered.com/news/2014/01/22/see-how-liberal-arts-grads-really-fare-report-examines-long-term-data

Chapter Summary and Highlights

This chapter catalogued and documented ten major benefits of a liberal arts education.
1. **Broadening personal interests and strengthening social self-confidence.** The breadth of knowledge and broadening perspectives acquired through the liberal arts expands your areas of personal interest and sources of mental stimulation

which, in turn, strengthens your social self-confidence. You'll be able to relate to a wider variety of people with a wider variety of educational, personal, and professional interests.

2. **Developing the capacity to learn effectively and efficiently.** Learning takes place when the brain makes a physical (neurological) connection between what you're trying to learn and something you already know—that is, something that's already stored in your brain. A liberal arts education increases the quantity and variety of neurological networks in your brain, thereby creating more pathways through which you can connect new ideas. This serves to (1) accelerate leaning by facilitating the connection-making process and (2) strengthen learning by enabling the connections to become more deeply rooted.

3. **Thinking critically from multiple perspectives.** Important world issues, problems, and challenges do not come tightly packaged in separated academic disciplines or subject areas; instead, they present themselves in the context of an interconnected, multiple-perspective system. Effective decision making and problem solving require "systems thinking"—understanding how our actions affect and are affected by other parts of a larger, interconnected system. This type of thinking underscores the importance of viewing issues from multiple perspectives, such as those developed by the liberal arts.

4. **Thinking creatively.** Studies show that creativity often emerges from a broad base of knowledge, perspectives, and skill sets that extend beyond the boundaries of a single, specialized field of study. Creative people have a wide range of interests and knowledge that typically crosses disciplinary boundaries, which enables them to draw on ideas from multiple subject areas. The variety of disciplines and perspectives developed by the liberal arts serves to stimulate creativity, enabling you to develop different thinking styles and strategies that can be mixed and matched to generate innovative ideas.

5. **Exploring and selecting college majors and career options.** Self-awareness is the critical first step toward making effective personal decisions and life choices. The breadth and depth of questions you're exposed to in the liberal arts will help you become more deeply aware of different dimen-

sions of yourself, including those that are critical for making effective decisions about majors and careers, such as (1) your interests—what you like to do, (2) your talents—what you have the ability to do well, and (3) your values—what you believe is important to do and is really worth doing.

6. **Acquiring skills for success in your college major.** General education isn't independent of or irrelevant to your major; the liberal arts represent the component of the college experience that provides the overall context and underlying skills needed for success in any specialized field of study. Although you may specialize in a particular field of study, real-life issues and challenges aren't conveniently divided into specialized majors and can neither be fully understood nor effectively solved with the thinking tools of a single academic discipline.

7. **Enhancing your career preparation and career success.** Today's employers are seeking workers with (1) communication skills: listening, speaking, writing, and reading; (2) thinking skills: critical thinking, creative thinking, and problem solving; and (3) lifelong learning skills: ability and willingness to learn continually throughout life. These skills and qualities are best developed by a well-rounded education that combines general education through the liberal arts and specialized education in a specific major. Interviews with hundreds of recent college graduates and employers indicate that both groups believe the best preparation for career entry is a college education that provides career-specific preparation plus broad-based knowledge and flexible skills—such as those developed by the liberal arts.

8. **Increasing your career options and occupational versatility.** Another way in which the liberal arts "liberate" you is by freeing you from narrow specialization; they increase your career options by equipping you with flexible work skills that are applicable to a wide range of work tasks and professional positions. These transferable skills increase your vocational freedom by increasing (1) initial options for career entry—your ability to enter different types of careers immediately after college, (2) career mobility—your ability to move from one career to another throughout the course of your career, and (3) opportunities for career reentry—your ability to move back into a career path after leaving it temporarily (e.g., to care for young children).

9. **Strengthening your prospects for career advancement and leadership.** Studies show that as the careers of college graduates progress, the narrower skills learned in their specialized major tend to decline in importance and are replaced by more general skills. Specialized skills provide you with *initial* job readiness, and in some careers, these specialized skills can be learned early through on-the-job training. Broad-based knowledge and general skills developed by the liberal arts, such as thinking and communicating, become more critical as you move up the career ladder.
10. **Educating you for life.** The liberal arts provide you with a set of skills that have two powerful qualities: (1) flexibility—portable skills that "travel well," which can be carried with you and applied across a wide range of work situations and life roles; and (2) durability—sustainable skills that have long-lasting value, which you can continue to use across changing times and different stages of life. You may forget much of the specialized, factual information learned in college; however, you will retain the ways of thinking, habits of mind, and communication skills developed by the liberal arts and will continue to use them in multiple life roles throughout life.

Questions and Final Reflections

1. In light of what you've read in this chapter, what points or arguments would you make to counter the claim that the liberal arts are impractical?

2. Explain how the broadening perspectives developed by the liberal arts are important for understanding and addressing *one* of the following problems:
   (a) War and terrorism
   (b) Poverty and hunger
   (c) Prejudice and discrimination
   (d) Developing sustainable energy
   (e) Any world issue of your choice

3. Rank the following in terms of their importance to you (1 = highest; 4 = lowest):
   ___ Getting a position with a high starting salary immediately after college (career entry)
   ___ Moving up in a career (career advancement)
   ___ Being able to move from one career to another (career mobility)
   ___ Being able to take time off from a career and return to it later (career re-entry)

What was your reasoning for choosing your *highest*-ranked item?

My *lowest*-ranked item was ranked last because . . .

4. In light of the ideas discussed in this chapter, how would you interpret or react to the following quotes?
   (a) "Employers do not want 'toothpick' graduates who have learned only the technical skills and who arrive in the workplace deep but narrow. These workers are sidelined early, employers report, because they cannot break out of their mental cubicles."
   —Association of American Colleges and Universities (2007)
   (b) "The illiterate of the 21st century will not be those who cannot read and write, but those who cannot learn, unlearn and relearn."
   —Alvin Toffler, author, *Rethinking the Future*
   (c) "Why do we go through the struggle to be educated? Is it merely to pass some examinations and get a job? Or is it the function of education to prepare us while we are young to understand the whole process of life?"
   —Jiddu Krishnamurti, author, *Think on These Things*

5. Complete the following sentences in a way that is most meaningful to you:
   (a) I would define *success* as . . . .
   (b) For me, a successful *career* is one that . . . .
   (c) To "live the good life" is to . . .

The Meaning and Purpose of Diversity

CHAPTER 3

PAUSE FOR THOUGHT

Please complete the following sentence:
When I hear the word "diversity," the first thoughts that come to mind are …

What Is Diversity?

Literally translated, the word "diversity" derives from the Latin root *diversus*, meaning "various" or "variety." Thus, human diversity refers to the variety that exists in humanity (the human species). The relationship between humanity and diversity is analogous to the relationship between sunlight and the variety of colors that make up the visual spectrum. Similar to how sunlight passing through a prism disperses into the variety of colors that comprise the visual spectrum, the human species inhabiting planet earth is dispersed into a variety of different groups that comprise the human spectrum (humanity). This metaphorical relationship between diversity and humanity is represented visually in **Figure 3.1**.

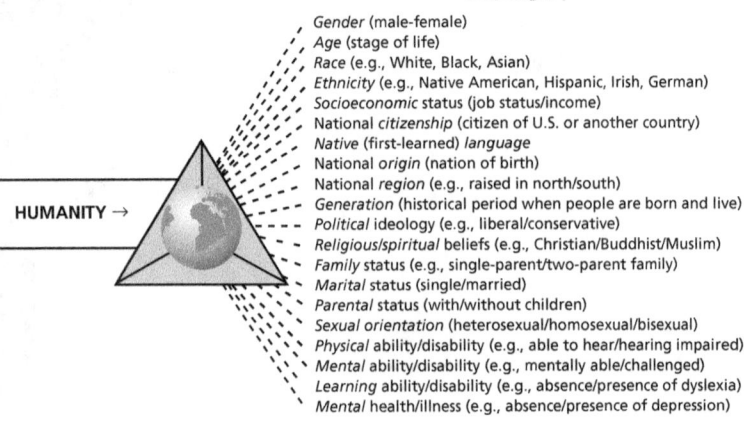

Humanity and Diversity

FIGURE 3.1

> "We are all brothers and sisters. Each face in the rainbow of color that populates our world is precious and special. Each adds to the rich treasure of humanity."
>
> —Morris Dees, civil rights leader and co-founder of the Southern Poverty Law Center

> "Ethnic and cultural diversity is an integral, natural, and normal component of educational experiences for all students."
>
> —National Council for Social Studies

As depicted in the figure, human diversity is manifested in a multiplicity of ways, including differences among human groups in terms of their physical features, national origins, cultural backgrounds, and sexual orientations. Some dimensions of diversity are easily detectable, others are more subtle, and some are invisible.

Diversity does involve pursuit of equal rights and social justice for minority groups, but it's a concept that involves much more than political issues. In a national survey of American voters, the vast majority of respondents agreed that diversity is more than just "political correctness" (215). Diversity is also an *educational* issue—an integral element of a liberal arts education that enhances learning, personal development, and career preparation of *all* students. It magnifies the

Humanity, Diversity, and the Liberal Arts: Foundation of a College Education

quality of the college experience by bringing multiple perspectives and alternative approaches to *what* is being learned (the content) and *how* it's being learned (the process).

KEY POINT

Diversity is a *human* issue that embraces and benefits *all* people; it's not a code word that stands for "some" people. Although one major goal of diversity is to promote appreciation and equitable treatment of particular groups of people who have experienced discrimination, it's also a *learning* experience that strengthens the quality of your college education, career preparation, and leadership potential.

What Is Racial Diversity?

A *racial group (race)* is a group of people who share distinctive physical traits, such as skin color or facial characteristics. The variations in skin color we now see among different humans are largely due to biological adaptations that have evolved over thousands of years among human groups who migrated to different climatic regions of the world. Currently, the most widely accepted explanation of the geographic origin of modern humans is the "Out of Africa" theory. Genetic studies and fossil evidence indicate that all Homo sapiens inhabited Africa 150,000 to 250,000 years ago; over time, some migrated from Africa to other parts of the world (190, 191, 248). Darker skin tones developed among humans who inhabited and reproduced in hotter geographical regions nearer the equator (e.g., Africans). Their darker skin color helped them adapt and survive by providing their bodies with better protection from the potentially damaging effects of intense sunlight (47). In contrast, lighter skin tones developed over time among humans inhabiting colder climates that were farther from the equator (e.g., Scandinavia). Their lighter skin color enabled their bodies to absorb greater amounts of vitamin D supplied by sunlight, which was in shorter supply in those regions of the world (150).

Currently, five races have been identified by the U.S. Census Bureau (284):

White—person whose lineage may be traced to the original people inhabiting Europe, the Middle East, or North Africa

Black or African American—person whose lineage may be traced to the original people inhabiting Africa

American Indian or Alaska Native—person whose lineage may be traced to the original people inhabiting North and South America (including Central America) who continue to maintain tribal affiliation or attachment

Asian—person whose lineage may be traced to the original people inhabiting the Far East, Southeast Asia, or the Indian subcontinent, including Cambodia, China, India, Japan, Korea, Malaysia, Pakistan, the Philippine Islands, Thailand, and Vietnam

Native Hawaiian or Other Pacific Islander—person whose lineage may be traced to the original people inhabiting Hawaii, Guam, Samoa, or other Pacific Islands

Racial categories, however, are not based on scientific evidence; they merely represent group classifications constructed by society (12). No identifiable set of genes distinguishes one race from another; in fact, there continues to be disagreement among scholars about what groups of people constitute a human race or whether distinctive races actually exist (292). In other words, you can't do a blood test or some type of internal genetic test to determine a person's race. Humans have simply decided to categorize themselves into races on the basis of certain external differences in their physical appearance, particularly the color of their outer layer of skin. The U.S. Census Bureau could have decided to divide people into "racial" categories based on other physical characteristics, such as eye color (blue, brown, and green) or hair color (brown, black, blonde, or red).

Author's Experience—Aaron Thompson

My father stood approximately six feet tall and had straight, light brown hair. His skin color was that of a Western European with a very slight suntan. My mother was from Alabama and she was dark in skin color with high cheekbones and long curly black hair. In fact, if you did not know that my father was of African American descent, you would not have thought of him as black.

All of my life I've thought of myself as African American and all people who know me have thought of me as African American. I have lived half of a century with that as my racial identity. Several years ago, I carefully reviewed records of births and deaths in my family history and discovered that I had fewer than 50 percent of African lineage. Biologically, I am no longer black; socially and emotionally, I still am. Clearly, my "race" has been socially constructed, not biologically determined.

While humans may display diversity in the color or tone of their external layer of skin, the reality is that all members of the human species are remarkably similar at an internal biological level. More than 98 percent of the genes of humans from all racial groups are exactly the same (47, 197). The large amount of genetic overlap among humans accounts for the many physical similarities that exist among us, despite the superficial differences in color appearing at the outer surface of our skin. We all have physical features that give us a "human" appearance and clearly distinguish us from other animal species. All humans have internal organs that are similar in structure and function, and despite variations in the color of our outer layer of skin, when it's cut, we all bleed in the same color.

Author's Experience—Joe Cuseo

I was sitting in a coffee shop in Chicago O'Hare airport while proofreading my first draft of this chapter. I looked up from my work for a second and saw what appeared to be a white girl about 18 years of age. As I lowered my head to return to work, I did a double-take and looked at her again because something about her seemed different or unusual. When I took a closer look at her the second time, I noticed that although she had white skin, the features of her face and hair appeared to be those of an African American. After a couple of seconds of puzzlement, I figured it out: she was an albino African American. That satisfied my curiosity for the moment, but then I began to wonder: Would it still be accurate to say she was "black" even though her skin was not black? Would her hair and facial features be sufficient for her to be considered or classified as black? If yes, then what would be the "race" of someone who had black skin tone, but did not have the typical hair and facial features characteristic of black people? Is skin color the defining feature of being African American or are other features equally important?

I was unable to answer these questions, but found it amusing that all of these thoughts were taking place while I was working on a chapter dealing with diversity. On the plane ride home, I thought again about that albino African American girl and realized that she was a perfect example of how classifying people into "races" is not based on objective, scientific evidence, but on subjective, socially constructed categories.

Furthermore, categorizing people into distinct racial or ethnic groups is becoming even more difficult because members of different ethnic and racial groups are increasingly forming cross-ethnic and interracial families. By 2050, the number of Americans who identify themselves as being of two or more races is projected to more than triple, growing from 5.2 million to 16.2 million (282).

Author's Experience—Aaron Thompson

In my current professional role, one of my responsibilities is to keep track of the racial and ethnic makeup of faculty, staff and students at the colleges and universities in my state. After the 2010 census, this became a harder task because many are reporting that they are members of multiple races and ethnicities. I'm beginning to realize that the more diverse we've become, the more similar we've all become. I may have to figure out a new way to calculate the racial and ethnic makeup of college students, faculty, and staff in my state!

PAUSE FOR THOUGHT

What race(s) do you consider yourself to be? Would you say you identify strongly with your racial identity, or are you rarely conscious of it? If yes, why? If no, why not?

What Is Cultural Diversity?

"Culture" may be defined as a distinctive pattern of beliefs and values learned by a group of people who share the same social heritage and traditions. In short, culture is the whole way in which a group of people has learned to live (236); it includes their style of speaking (language), fashion, food, art and music, as well as their beliefs and values.

Sometimes, the terms "culture" and "society" are used interchangeably as if they were synonymous; however, these concepts refer to different aspects of humanity. *Society* refers to a group of people who are organized under the same social system. For example, all members of American society are organized under the same system of government, justice, and education. *Culture*, on the other hand, is what members of a certain group of people actually have in common with respect to their traditions and lifestyle (219). Thus, groups of people living in the same society may still be culturally different if they have different social traditions and customs. For instance Asian Americans and African Americans live under the same social system, but have different cultures. Thus, cultural differences can exist within the same society (multicultural society) just as cultural differences exist across different nations (cross-cultural or international diversity).

It could be said that the academic divisions of knowledge comprising the liberal arts curriculum represent different components of human culture that scholars have decided to specialize in and study systematically. Thus, by studying a variety of academic disciplines, you become "cultured" or a person "of culture." **Box 3.1** contains a summary of key components of culture that a group may share. Notice how these cultural components correspond closely to the content covered and questions asked by different fields of study in the liberal arts.

PAUSE FOR THOUGHT

Look back at the components of culture cited in Box 3.1. Add another aspect of culture to the list that you think is important or influential. Explain why you think this is an important element of culture.

BOX 3.1

Key Components of Culture

Language—how members of the culture communicate through written or spoken words, their particular dialect, and their style of nonverbal communication (body language)

Space—how cultural members arrange themselves with respect to social–spatial distance (e.g., how closely they stand next to each other when conversing)

Time—how the culture conceives of, divides, and uses time (e.g., the speed or pace at which they conduct business)

Aesthetics—how cultural members appreciate and express artistic beauty and creativity (e.g., their style of visual art, culinary art, music, theater, literature, and dance)

Family—the culture's attitudes and habits with respect to interacting with parents and children (e.g., customary styles of parenting and caring for elderly family members)

Economics—how the culture meets its members' material needs and its customary ways of acquiring and distributing wealth (e.g., the gap between the very rich and very poor)

Gender roles—the culture's expectations for "appropriate" male and female behavior (e.g., whether or not women are able to hold the same leadership positions as men)

Politics—how decision-making power is exercised in the culture (e.g., democratically or autocratically)

Science and technology—the culture's attitude toward and use of science or technology (e.g., the degree to which the culture is technologically "advanced")

Philosophy—the culture's ideas or views on wisdom, goodness, truth, and social values (e.g., whether they place greater value on individual competition or collective collaboration)

Spirituality and religion—cultural beliefs about a supreme being and an afterlife (e.g., its predominant faith-based views and belief systems about the supernatural)

> **Author's Experience—Joe Cuseo**
>
> *I was watching a basketball game between the Los Angeles Lakers and Los Angeles Clippers when a short scuffle broke out between the Lakers' Paul Gasol—who is Spanish, and the Clippers' Chris Paul—who is African American. After the scuffle ended, Gasol tried to show Paul there were no hard feelings by patting him on the head. Instead of interpreting Gasol's head pat as a peace-making gesture, Paul took it as a putdown and returned the favor by slapping (rather than patting) Paul in the head!*
>
> *This whole misunderstanding stemmed from a basic difference in nonverbal communication between the two cultures. Patting someone on the head in European cultures is a friendly gesture; European soccer players often do it to an opposing player to express no ill will after a foul or collision. However, this same nonverbal message meant something very different to Chris Paul—an African American who was raised in urban America.*

What Is an Ethnic Group?

A group of people who share the same culture is referred to as an *ethnic group*. Thus, "culture" refers to *what* an ethnic group shares in common (e.g., language and traditions) and "ethnic group" refers to the *people* who share a culture that has been *learned* through common social experiences. Members of the same racial group—whose shared physical characteristics have been *inherited*—may be members of different ethnic groups. For instance, white Americans belong to the same racial group, but differ in terms of their ethnic group (e.g., French, German, Irish) and Asian Americans belong to the same racial group, but are members of different ethnic groups (e.g., Japanese, Chinese, Korean). It's noteworthy that members of ethnic minority groups who are white can more easily "blend into" or assimilate into society because their minority status cannot be easily identified by the color of their skin. In fact, to further accelerate their assimilation into American culture and acquire the privileges of the majority group, a number of white minority immigrants of European ancestry changed their last name to appear to be Americans of English descent. In contrast, the immediately detectable minority status of African Americans, darker-skinned Hispanics, and Native Americans didn't allow them the option of presenting themselves as members of an already-assimilated majority group (212).

Currently, the major cultural (ethnic) groups in the United States include:
- Native Americans (American Indians)
  - Cherokee, Navaho, Hopi, Alaskan Natives, Blackfoot, for example
- European Americans (Whites)
  - Descendents from Western Europe (e.g., United Kingdom, Ireland, Netherlands), Eastern Europe (e.g., Hungary, Romania, Bulgaria), Southern Europe (e.g., Italy, Greece, Portugal), and Northern Europe or Scandinavia (e.g., Denmark, Sweden, Norway)
- African Americans (Blacks)
  - Americans whose cultural roots lie in the continent of Africa (e.g., Ethiopia, Kenya, Nigeria) and the Caribbean Islands (e.g., Bahamas, Cuba, Jamaica)
- Hispanic Americans (Latinos)
  - Americans with cultural roots in Mexico, Puerto Rico, Central America (e.g., El Salvador, Guatemala, Nicaragua), and South America (e.g., Brazil, Columbia, Venezuela)
- Asian Americans
  - Americans whose cultural roots lie in East Asia (e.g., Japan, China, Korea), Southeast Asia (e.g., Vietnam, Thailand, Cambodia), and South Asia (e.g., India, Pakistan. Bangladesh)
- Middle Eastern Americans
  - For example, Americans with cultural roots in Iraq, Iran, and Israel

PAUSE FOR THOUGHT

What ethnic group(s) are you a member of, or do you identify with? What would you say are the key cultural values shared by your ethnic group(s)?

CHAPTER 3: The Meaning and Purpose of Diversity

European Americans are still the majority ethnic group in the United States; they account for more than 50 percent of the American population. Native Americans, African Americans, Hispanic Americans, and Asian Americans are considered to be *minority* ethnic groups because each of these groups represents less than 50 percent of the American population. America's two most populated states, California and Texas, are called "minority-majority" states because more than half of the population in these states is now comprised of people from minority groups; the same is true for Hawaii and New Mexico (282). As with racial grouping, classifying humans into different ethnic groups can be very arbitrary and subject to debate. Currently, the U.S. Census Bureau classifies Hispanics as an ethnic group rather than a race. However, among Americans who checked "some other race" in the 2000 Census, 97 percent were Hispanic. This finding suggests that Hispanic Americans consider themselves to be a racial group, probably because that's how they feel they're perceived and treated by non-Hispanics (70). It's revealing that the American media used the term "racial profiling" (rather than ethnic profiling) to describe Arizona's controversial 2010 law that allowed police to target Hispanics who "look" like illegal aliens from Mexico, Central America, and South America. Once again, this illustrates how race and ethnicity are subjective, socially constructed concepts that reflect how people perceive and treat certain social groups, which, in turn, affects how members of these groups perceive themselves.

> "I'm the only person from my race in class."
>
> —Hispanic student commenting on why he felt comfortable in his class on race, ethnicity, and gender

The racial and ethnic diversity in our nation is accompanied by sharp economic differences across minority and majority groups. In 2012, the median income for non-Hispanic white households was $57,009, compared to $39,005 for Hispanics and $33,321 for African Americans (92). From 2005 to 2009, household wealth fell by 66 percent for Hispanics, 53 percent for blacks, and 16 percent for whites, largely due to the housing and mortgage collapse—which had a more damaging effect on lower-income families (169).

> "You can have a democracy and a society sharply divided between the rich and the poor, but you cannot have both for very long."
>
> —Louis Brandeis, former Supreme Court justice

The Relationship between Diversity and Humanity

As mentioned earlier, diversity represents variations on the same theme: being human. Humanity and diversity are interdependent, complementary concepts. To understand human diversity is to understand both our differences and *similarities* (246). Diversity appreciation includes appreciating the unique perspectives of different groups of people as well as the universal aspects of the human experience that are common to all groups. Regardless of our ethnic or racial group, we all live in communities, develop relationships, have emotional needs, and undergo life experiences that affect our self-esteem and personal identity. All humans also share a number of other common characteristics and experiences, such as being citizens of the same nation, persons of the same gender, and members of the same generation. In addition, humans of all races and ethnicities experience and express the same human emotions, and they communicate those emotions with the same facial expressions (see **Figure 3.2**).

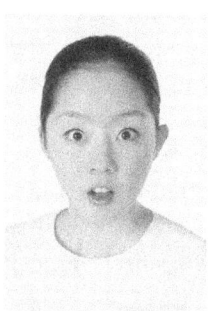

FIGURE 3.2

Humans all over the world display the same facial expressions when experiencing and expressing different emotions. See if you can detect the emotions being expressed in these faces. (To find the answers, turn your book upside down.)

Answers: The emotions shown, Top, left to right: anger, fear, and sadness. Bottom, left to right: disgust, happiness, and surprise.

PAUSE FOR THOUGHT

List three human experiences that you think are universal—which are experienced by humans of all racial and ethnic groups.

1.

2.

3.

Other characteristics that anthropologists have found to be shared by all humans in every corner of the world include storytelling, poetry, adornment of the body, dance, music, decoration with artifacts, families, socialization of children by elders, a sense of right and wrong, supernatural beliefs, and mourning of the dead (242). Although different cultural groups may express these shared experiences in different ways, these universal experiences are common to all human cultures.

The interdependent relationship between humanity and diversity is well illustrated by language development in humans. Cultural groups around the world speak different languages characterized by distinctively different sounds; yet, when all human babies are born, they babble in sounds used in all human languages. This gives every newborn human being the potential to speak the sounds of any human language to which he or she is exposed. Over time, newborns will only continue to use the sounds they hear spoken by their particular cultural group; the babbling sounds they made in other languages will eventually drop out of their oral repertoire if they don't hear those sounds spoken by member of the culture in which they're raised (227). The same set of sounds we all used at birth reflects our common humanity (the universal "human language"); the particular set of sounds we heard as infants and learned to speak (our "native language") reflects our cultural diversity.

You may have heard the question: "We're all human, aren't we?" The answer to this important question is "yes and no." Yes, we're all the same, but not in the same way. A good metaphor for understanding this apparent contradiction is to visualize human groups as a quilt in which we're all united by the common thread of humanity—the universal bond of being human (see **Figure 3.3**). The different patches comprising the quilt represent diversity—the distinctive or unique cultures that comprise our common humanity. The quilt metaphor acknowledges the identity and beauty of all cultures. It differs from the old American "melting pot" metaphor, which viewed cultural differences as something that should be melted down and eliminated. It also differs from the old "salad bowl" metaphor that suggested America was a hodgepodge or mishmash of cultures thrown together without any common connection. In contrast, the quilt metaphor suggests that the unique cultures of different human groups should be preserved, recognized, and valued; at the same time, these cultural differences join together to form a seamless, unified whole. This blending of diversity and unity is captured in the Latin expression *E pluribus unum* ("Out of many, one")—the motto of the United States—which you'll find printed on all of its coins.

"We are all the same, and we are all unique."

—Georgia Dunston, African American biologist and research specialist in human genetics

KEY POINT

When we appreciate diversity in the context of humanity, we capitalize on the variety and versatility of human differences while preserving the collective strength and synergy of human unity.

"We have become not a melting pot but a beautiful mosaic."

—Jimmy Carter, thirty-ninth president of the United States and winner of the Nobel Peace Prize

Different patches comprising the quilt represent diversity.

FIGURE 3.3

> **Author's Experience—Joe Cuseo**
>
> *When I was 12 years old and living in New York City, I returned from school one Friday and my mother asked me if anything interesting happened at school that day. I told her that the teacher went around the room asking students what we had for dinner the night before. At that moment, my mother became a bit concerned and nervously asked me: "What did you tell the teacher?" I said: "I told her and the rest of the class that I had pasta last night because my family always eats pasta on Thursdays and Sundays." My mother exploded and fired back at me, "Why didn't you tell her we had steak or roast beef?!" For a moment, I was stunned and couldn't figure out what I'd done wrong or why I should have lied about eating pasta. Then it dawned on me: My mom was embarrassed about being Italian American. She wanted me to hide our family's ethnic background and make it sound like we were very "American."*
>
> *As I grew older, I understood why my mother felt the way she did. She grew up in America's "melting pot" generation—a time when different American ethnic groups were expected to melt down and melt away their ethnicity. They were not to celebrate their diversity; they were to eliminate it.*

What Is Individuality?

It's important to keep in mind that individual differences among members of any racial or ethnic group are greater than the average difference between groups. Said in another way, there's more variability (individuality) within groups than between groups. For example, among members of the same racial group, individual differences in their physical attributes (e.g., height and weight) and psychological characteristics (e.g., temperament and personality) are greater than any average difference that may exist between their racial group and other racial groups (63).

KEY POINT

While it's valuable to learn about differences between different human groups, there are substantial individual differences among people within the same racial or ethnic group that should neither be ignored nor overlooked. Don't assume that individuals with the same racial or ethnic characteristics share the same personal characteristics.

"I realize that I'm black, but I like to be viewed as a person, and this is everybody's wish."

—Michael Jordan, Hall of Fame basketball player

As you proceed through your college experience, keep the following key distinctions in mind (**Figure 3.4**):

- **Humanity**—All humans are members of the *same group*—the human species.
- **Diversity**—All humans are members of *different groups* (e.g., different racial and ethnic groups).
- **Individuality**—Each human is a *unique individual* who differs from all other members of any group to which he or she may belong.

"Every human is, at the same time, like all other humans, like some humans, and like no other human."

—Clyde Kluckholn, American anthropologist

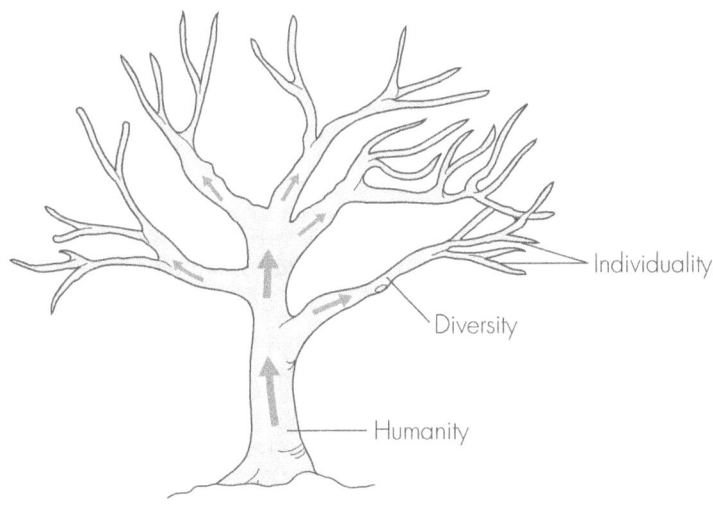

The Relationship between Humanity, Diversity, and Individuality

FIGURE 3.4

CHAPTER 3: The Meaning and Purpose of Diversity

What Is Ethnocentrism?

A major advantage of culture is it promotes group solidarity, binding its members into a supportive, tight-knit community. Unfortunately, however, culture not only serves to bind us, it can also blind us from taking different cultural perspectives. Since culture shapes thought and perception, people from the same ethnic (cultural) group run the risk of becoming *ethnocentric*—centered on their own culture to such a degree that they view the world solely through their own cultural lens (frame of reference) and fail to consider or appreciate other cultural perspectives (74).

Optical illusions are a good example of how our particular cultural perspective can influence (and distort) our perceptions. Compare the lengths of the two lines in **Figure 3.5**.

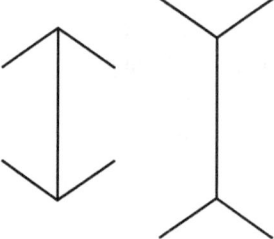

Optical Illusion

FIGURE 3.5

If you perceive the line on the right to be longer than the one on the left, your perception has been shaped by Western culture. People from other Western cultures perceive the line on the right to be longer; however, both lines are actually equal in length. (If you don't believe it, take out a ruler and measure them.) Interestingly, this perceptual error isn't made by people from non-Western cultures whose living spaces and architectural structures are predominantly circular (e.g., huts or igloos), rather than the rectangular-shaped buildings with angled corners that typify Western cultures (254).

People whose cultural experience involve living and working in circular structures would not be fooled by the optical illusion in Figure 3.5.

The optical illusion depicted in Figure 3.5 is just one of a number of illusions that are experienced by people in certain cultures, but not others (260). These cross-cultural differences in susceptibility to optical illusions illustrate how strongly our cultural experiences can influence and sometimes misinform our perception of reality. People think they are seeing things objectively—as they actually are, but they're really seeing things subjectively—as viewed from their particular cultural perspective.

If our prior cultural experience can influence our perception of the physical world, it can certainly shape our interpretation of social events and political issues. In fact, psychological research indicates that what is more familiar to us is often perceived to be better than the unfamiliar. The more exposure humans have to somebody or something, the more familiar it becomes and the more likely it will be perceived positively and judged favorably. The effect of familiarity is so prevalent and powerful that social psychologists have come to call it the "familiarity principle"—that is, what is familiar is perceived as better or more acceptable (296, 297, 298).

CHAPTER 3: The Meaning and Purpose of Diversity

We need to be mindful of the subjectivity of our own cultural perspective and the bias associated with cultural familiarity. By remaining open to the viewpoints of people who perceive the world from different cultural vantage points, we minimize our cultural blind spots, expand our range of perception, and position ourselves to perceive the world around us with greater comprehensiveness, clarity, and cultural sensitivity.

What Is Stereotyping?

"Stereotype" derives from two different word roots: *stereo*—to look at in a fixed way, and *type*—to categorize or group together, as in the word "typical." Thus, to stereotype is to view individuals of the same type (group) in the same (fixed) way.

Stereotyping ignores or disregards individuality; all people sharing the same group characteristic (e.g., race or gender) tend to be viewed as having the same personal characteristics—as reflected in the expression, "You know how they are; they're all alike." Stereotypes also involve *bias*—which literally means "slant"—a slant that can lean toward the positive or the negative. Positive bias results in favorable stereotypes (e.g., "Asians are great in science and math"); negative bias leads to unfavorable stereotypes (e.g., "Asians are nerds who do nothing but study"). Here are some other examples of negative stereotypes:

- Muslims are religious fanatics.
- Whites can't jump (or dance).
- Blacks are lazy.
- Irish are alcoholics.
- Gay men are feminine; lesbian women are masculine.
- Jews are cheap.
- Women are weak.

While few people would agree with these crass stereotypes, most people do make subtle assumptions about members of different groups. Such assumptions can malign the identity of a group, deprive its members of their individuality, and undermine their prospects for success.

Author's Experience—Aaron Thompson

When I was 6 years old, I was told by a 6-year-old girl from a different racial group that all people of my race could not swim. Since I couldn't swim at that time and she could, I assumed she was correct. I asked a boy, who was a member of the same racial group as the girl, whether her statement was true. He responded emphatically: "Yes, it's true!" Since I was from an area where few other African Americans were around to counteract this belief about my racial group, I continued to buy into this stereotype until I finally took swimming lessons as an adult. After many lessons, I am now a lousy swimmer because I didn't even attempt to swim until I was an adult. The moral of this story is that group stereotypes can limit the confidence and potential of individual members of the stereotyped group.

Whether you're male or female, don't let gender stereotypes limit your personal potential or career options.

CHAPTER 3: The Meaning and Purpose of Diversity

PAUSE FOR THOUGHT

1. Have you ever been stereotyped based on your appearance or group membership? If so, how did it make you feel and how did you react?
2. Have you ever unintentionally perceived or treated a person in terms of a group stereotype rather than as an individual? What assumptions did you make about that person? Was that person aware of, or affected by, your stereotyping?

"The best way to beat prejudice is to show them. On a midterm, I got 40 points above the average. They all looked at me differently after that" (216).

—Mexican-American student

"See that man over there? Yes.
Well, I hate him.
But you don't know him.
That's why I hate him."

—Gordon Allport, influential social psychologist and author of *The Nature of Prejudice*

What Is Prejudice?

If virtually all members of a stereotyped group are judged and evaluated in a negative way, the result is *prejudice*. (The word "prejudice" literally means to "pre-judge.") Technically, prejudice may be either positive or negative; however, the term is most often associated with a negative prejudgment that involves *stigmatizing*—ascribing inferior or unfavorable traits to people who belong to the same group. Thus, prejudice may be defined as a negative stereotype held about a group of people that's formed before the facts are known.

Someone holding a group prejudice typically avoids contact with individuals from that group. This enables the prejudice to continue unchallenged because there's little opportunity for the prejudiced person to have positive experiences with a member of the stigmatized group that could contradict or disprove the prejudice. Thus, a vicious cycle is established in which the prejudiced person continues to avoid contact with individuals from the stigmatized group; this, in turn, continues to maintain and reinforce the person's prejudice.

What Is Discrimination?

Literally translated, the term "discrimination" means "division" or "separation." Whereas prejudice involves a belief, attitude, or opinion, discrimination involves an *action* or *behavior*. Technically, discrimination can be either positive or negative. A discriminating eater may only eat healthy foods, which is a positive quality. However, discrimination is most often associated with a harmful act that results in a prejudiced person treating another individual, or group of individuals, in an unfair way. Thus, it could be said that discrimination is prejudice put into action. For instance, to fire or not hire people on the basis of their race, gender, or sexual orientation is an act of discrimination.

Box 3. 2 contains a summary of the major forms of discrimination, prejudice, and stereotypes that have plagued humanity. As you read through the list, note whether you, a friend, or family member experienced any of these forms of prejudice.

> **BOX 3.2**
>
> **Stereotypes, Prejudices, and Forms of Discrimination**
>
> * **Ethnocentrism**—viewing one's own culture or ethnic group as "central" or "normal," while viewing different cultures as "deficient" or "inferior"
>   Example: viewing another culture as "abnormal" or "uncivilized" because its members eat animals that our culture considers unethical to eat, even though we eat animals their culture considers unethical to eat
> * **Stereotyping**—viewing all (or virtually all) members of the same group in the same way—that is, as having the same personal qualities or characteristics
>   Example: "If you're Italian, you must be in the Mafia, or have a family member who is."
> * **Prejudice**—having negative prejudgment about another group of people
>   Example: Women can't be effective leaders because they're too emotional.

> "Let us all hope that the dark clouds of racial prejudice will soon pass away and ... in some not too distant tomorrow the radiant stars of love and brotherhood will shine over our great nation."
>
> —Martin Luther King, Jr., civil rights leader, humanitarian, and youngest recipient of the Nobel Peace Prize

* **Discrimination**—displaying unequal and unfair treatment of a person or group of people—that is, prejudice put into action
  Example: paying women less than men for performing the same job, even though they have the same level of education and job qualifications
* **Segregation**—making an intentional group decision to separate the group (socially or physically) from another group
  Example: "White flight"—white people moving out of neighborhoods when people of color move in
* **Racism**—holding a belief that one's racial group is superior to another group and expressing that belief in an attitude (prejudice) or action (discrimination)
  Example: confiscating land from Native Americans based on the unfounded belief that they are "uncivilized" or "savages"
* **Institutional racism**—practicing racism rooted in organizational policies and practices that disadvantage certain racial groups
  Example: race-based discrimination in mortgage lending, housing and bank loans
* **Racial profiling**—investigating or arresting someone solely on the basis of the person's race, ethnicity, or national origin, without witnessing actual criminal behavior or having incriminating evidence
  Example: police making a traffic stop or conducting a personal search based solely on an individual's racial features
* **Slavery**—using forced labor in which people are considered to be property, held against their will, and deprived of the right to leave or receive wages
  Example: enslavement of Blacks, which was legal in the United States until 1865.
* **"Jim Crow laws"**—formal and informal laws created by whites to segregate blacks after the abolition of slavery
  Example: laws in certain parts of the United States that once required blacks to use separate bathrooms and be educated in separate schools.

* **Apartheid**—an institutionalized system of "legal racism" supported by a nation's government (Apartheid derives from a word in the Afrikaan language, meaning "apartness.")
  Example: South Africa's national system of racial segregation and discrimination that was in place from 1948 to 1994
* **Hate crimes**—criminal action motivated solely by prejudice toward the crime victim
  Example: acts of vandalism or assault aimed at members of a particular ethnic group or persons with a particular sexual orientation
* **Hate groups**—organizations whose primary purpose is to stimulate prejudice, discrimination, or aggression toward certain groups of people based on their ethnicity, race, religion, etc.
  Example: Ku Klux Klan—an American terrorist group that perpetrates hatred toward all non-white races
* **Genocide**—mass murdering of a particular ethnic or racial group
  Example: the Holocaust, in which millions of Jews were systematically murdered during World War II. Other examples include the murdering of Cambodians under the Khmer Rouge regime, the murdering of Bosnian Muslims in the former country of Yugoslavia, and the slaughter of the Tutsi minority by the Hutu majority in Rwanda.
* **Classism**—showing prejudice or discrimination based on social class, particularly toward people of lower socioeconomic status
  Example: acknowledging the contributions made by politicians and wealthy industrialists to America, while ignoring the contributions of poor immigrants, farmers, slaves, and pioneer women
* **Religious intolerance**—denying the fundamental human right of people to hold religious beliefs, or to hold religious beliefs that differ from one's own
  Example: an atheist who forces non-religious (secular) beliefs on others, or a member of a religious group who believes that people who hold different religious beliefs are infidels or "sinners" whose souls will not be saved

"Never, never, and never again shall it be that this beautiful land will again experience the oppression of one by another."

—Nelson Mandela, anti-Apartheid revolutionary, first black president of South Africa after Apartheid, and winner of the Nobel Peace Prize

"Most religions dictate that theirs is the only way, and without believing in it, you cannot enter the mighty kingdom of heaven. Who are we to judge? It makes more sense for God to be the only one mighty enough to make that decision."

—First-year college student

CHAPTER 3: The Meaning and Purpose of Diversity

> "Rivers, ponds, lakes and streams— they all have different names, but they all contain water. Just as religions do— they all contain truths."
>
> —Muhammad Ali, three-time world heavyweight boxing champion, member of the International Boxing Hall of Fame, and recipient of the Spirit of America Award as the most recognized American in the world

> "Facts do not cease to exist because they are ignored."
>
> –Aldous Huxley, English writer and author of Brave New World

> "Above all nations is humanity."
>
> —Motto of the University of Hawaii

* **Anti-Semitism**—showing prejudice or discrimination toward Jews or people who practice the religion of Judaism
Example: disliking Jews because they're the ones who "killed Christ"
* **Xenophobia**—having an extreme fear or hatred of foreigners, outsiders, or strangers
Example: believing that all immigrants should be banned from entering the country because they will undermine our economy and increase our crime rate
* **Regional bias**—showing prejudice or discrimination based on the geographical region in which an individual was born and raised.
Example: a Northerner thinking that all Southerners are racists
* **Dogmatism**—stubbornly clinging to a personally held viewpoint that's unsupported by evidence and remaining closed minded (non-receptive) to other viewpoints that are better supported by evidence
Example: people who insist that America's form of capitalism is the only economic system that can work in a successful democracy, and refusing to acknowledge the fact that other successful democratic countries use different forms of capitalism
* **Jingoism**—having excessive interest and belief in the superiority of one's own nation without acknowledging its mistakes or weaknesses, often accompanied by an aggressive foreign policy that neglects the needs of other nations, or the common needs of all nations
Example: "Blind patriotism"—not seeing the shortcomings of one's own nation and viewing any questioning or criticism of one's own nation as being disloyal or "unpatriotic" (as in the slogan, "America: right or wrong" or "America: love it or leave it!")
* **Terrorism**—committing intentional acts of violence against civilians which are motivated by political or religious prejudice
Example: the September 11, 2001, attacks on the United States

* **Sexism**—showing prejudice or discrimination based on sex or gender
  Example: believing that women should not pursue careers in fields traditionally filled only by men (e.g., engineering or political leadership) because they lack the innate qualities or skills to do so
* **Heterosexism**—holding the belief that heterosexuality is the only acceptable sexual orientation
  Example: believing that gays should not have the same legal rights and opportunities as heterosexuals
* **Homophobia**—having extreme fear or hatred of homosexuals
  Example: creating or contributing to anti-gay Web sites, or "gay bashing" (acts of violence toward gays)
* **Ageism**—showing prejudice or discrimination toward certain age groups, particularly toward the elderly
  Example: believing that all "old" people have dementia and shouldn't be allowed to make decisions that affect others
* **Ableism**—showing prejudice or discrimination toward people who are disabled or handicapped (physically, mentally, or emotionally)
  Example: intentionally avoiding social contact with people in wheelchairs

PAUSE FOR THOUGHT

As you read through the list in Box 3.2, did you note if you, a friend, or family member experienced any of the form(s) of prejudice listed? If yes, what happened and why do you think it happened?

Once prejudice has been formed, it often remains intact and resistant to change through the psychological process of *selective perception*—the tendency for biased (prejudiced) people to see what they *expect* to see and fail to see what contradicts their bias (143). Have you ever noticed how fans rooting for their favorite sports team tend to focus on and "see" the calls of referees that go against their own team, but don't seem to react or even notice many calls that go against the opposing team? This is a classic example of selective perception. In effect, selective perception transforms the old adage, "seeing is believing," into "believing is seeing." This can lead prejudiced people to focus their attention on information that's consistent with their prejudgment, causing them to "see" information that supports or reinforces it and ignore or overlook information that contradicts it.

> "We see what is behind our eyes."
>
> —Chinese proverb

Making matters worse, selective perception is often accompanied by *selective memory*—the tendency to remember information that's consistent with one's prejudicial belief and forget information that's inconsistent with it or contradicts it (154). The dual mental processes of selective perception and selective memory often work together and operate *unconsciously*. As a result, prejudiced people may not even be aware they're using these biased mental processes or realize how these processes are keeping their prejudice permanently in place (26).

> "A very bad (and all too common) way to misread a newspaper: To see whatever supports your point of view as fact, and anything that contradicts your point of view as bias."
>
> —Daniel Okrent, first public editor of *The New York Times* and inventor of Rotisserie League Baseball, the best-known form of fantasy baseball

PAUSE FOR THOUGHT

Have you witnessed selective perception or selective memory—people seeing or recalling what they believe is true (due to bias), rather than what is true? If yes, what happened and why do you think it happened?

Prejudice can occur without full conscious awareness. The first step in the process of appreciating diversity is developing self-awareness about our beliefs and attitudes toward differences, particularly awareness of any stereotypes or prejudices we may have that are biasing our perception of, or behavior toward, different groups of people, whether that bias is conscious or unconscious, intentional or unintentional, overt or covert.

As discussed in earlier chapters, the liberal arts develop skills for self-awareness, critical thinking, and multiple perspective-taking—the very skills needed to combat the type of biased and ethnocentric thinking that underlies stereotyping, prejudice, and discrimination (234). This illustrates how a liberal arts education and diversity appreciation are intertwined, mutually reinforcing learning processes. In the next chapter, the symbiotic relationship between the liberal arts and diversity will be examined in greater detail.

Internet Resources

For additional information related to the ideas discussed in this chapter, see the following websites:

Stereotyping: ReducingStereotypeThreat.org:
    www.reducingstereotypethreat.org/
Prejudice and Discrimination: Teaching Tolerance.Org:
    www.tolerance.org/
Human Rights: Amnesty International:
    www.amnesty.org/en/discrimination
Sexism in the Media: "Killing Us Softly":
    www.youtube.com/watch?v=PTlmho_RovY
LGBT Acceptance and Support: It Gets Better Project:
    www.itgetsbetter.org/

Chapter Summary and Highlights

Human diversity refers to the variety that exists in humanity (the human species). Diversity does involve pursuit of equal rights and social justice for minority groups, but it's a concept that involves much more than political issues. It's also an educational issue—an integral element of a liberal arts education that enhances learning, personal development, and career preparation of all students. Diversity is a human issue that involves all people; it's not a code word that stands for "some" people.

Racial diversity refers to groups of people who share distinctive physical traits, such as skin color or facial characteristics. Currently, five races have been identified by the U.S. Census Bureau: White, Black or African American, American Indian or Alaska Native, Asian, and Native Hawaiian or Other Pacific Islander. However, racial categories are not based on scientific evidence; they merely represent group classifications constructed by society. No identifiable set of genes distinguishes one race from another; in fact, there continues to be disagreement among scholars about what groups of people constitute a human race or whether distinctive races actually exist.

Cultural diversity refers to differences among groups of people who have a distinctive pattern of beliefs and values that were learned through sharing the same social heritage and traditions. In short, culture is the whole way in which a group of people has learned to live; it includes their style of speaking (language), fashion, food, art and music, as well as their beliefs and values. It could be said that the academic divisions of knowledge comprising the liberal arts curriculum represent different components of human culture that scholars have decided to specialize in and study systematically. Thus, by studying a variety of academic disciplines, you become "cultured" or a person "of culture."

A group of people who share the same culture is referred to as an *ethnic group*. Thus, "culture" refers to *what* an ethnic group shares in common (e.g., language and traditions) and "ethnic group" refers to the *people* who share a culture that has been *learned* through common social experiences. European Americans are still the majority ethnic group in the United States; they account for more than 50 percent of the American population. Native Americans, African Americans, Hispanic Americans, and Asian Americans are considered to be *minority* ethnic groups because each of these groups represents less than 50 percent of the American population.

Diversity represents variations on the same theme: being human. Humanity and diversity are interdependent, complementary concepts. To understand human diversity is to understand both our differences and *similarities.* Diversity appreciation includes appreciating the unique perspectives of different groups of people as well as the universal aspects of the human experience that are common to all groups—whatever their particular racial or cultural background happens to be. When we appreciate diversity in the context of humanity, we capitalize on the variety and versatility of human differences while preserving the collective strength and synergy of human unity.

While it's valuable to learn about differences between different human groups, there are substantial individual differences among people within the same racial or ethnic group that should neither be ignored nor overlooked. In short, it's important to keep three key distinctions in mind: (1) *humanity*—**a**ll humans are members of the same group—the human species; (2) *diversity*—all humans are members of different groups (e.g., different racial and ethnic groups; and (3) *individuality*—each human is a unique individual who differs from all other members of any group to which he or she may belong.

Ethnocentrism refers to when people become centered on their own culture to such a degree that they view the world solely through their own cultural lens (frame of reference) and fail to consider or appreciate other cultural perspectives. We need to be mindful of the subjectivity of our own cultural perspective and the bias associated with cultural familiarity. By remaining open to the viewpoints of people who perceive the world from different cultural vantage points, we minimize our cultural blind spots, expand our range of perception, and position ourselves to perceive the world around us with greater comprehensiveness, clarity, and cultural sensitivity.

Stereotyping refers to viewing individuals of the same type (group) in the same (fixed) way. Stereotypes ignore or disregard individuality; all people sharing the same group characteristic (e.g., race or gender) tend to be viewed as having the same personal characteristics. If virtually all members of a stereotyped group are judged and evaluated in a negative way, the result is *prejudice*. Thus, prejudice may be defined as "a negative stereotype held about a group of people that's formed before the facts are known." *Discrimination* involves an action or behavior that results in a prejudiced person treating another individual, or group of individuals, in an unfair way. Thus, it could be said that discrimination is prejudice put into action.

Stereotyping, prejudice, and discrimination stem from lack of self-awareness, critical thinking, and multiple perspective-taking. The liberal arts equip you with skills in each of these three areas, enabling you to combat the type of biased and ethnocentric thinking that underlies stereotyping, prejudice, and discrimination.

Questions and Final Reflections

1. Review the list of groups contained in the diversity spectrum in Figure 3.1.
   Think of another group to add to the list. Why would you add this group?

2. If you were to be born again as a member of a different racial or ethnic group:
   (a) What group would you choose? Why?
   (b) With your new group identity, what things would change in your personal life? What things would remain the same despite the fact that your group identity has changed?
   (c) What group would you not want to be born into? Why?

3. In light of the ideas discussed in this chapter, how would you interpret or react to the following quotes?
   (a) "Every human is, at the same time, like all other humans, like some humans, and like no other human."
   —Clyde Kluckholn, American anthropologist

(b) "We see what is behind our eyes."
—Chinese proverb

(c) "A comparison of American cultural products, practices, and perspectives to those of another culture will lead to a more profound understanding of what it means to be an American."
—David Conley, author, *College Knowledge*

4. Review the different components of culture in Box 3.1. Select one and describe how American culture differs from other cultures with respect to this component. What do you see are the major advantages and limitations of this aspect of American culture?

5. How would you interpret the meaning of the following expressions?
   (a) "That's so ghetto."
   (b) "White trash."

Would you say either of these expressions is offensive, biased, or prejudicial in any way?
If yes, why? If no, why not?

The Relationship between Liberal Arts and Diversity

CHAPTER 4

PAUSE FOR THOUGHT

Do you see any commonality or connection between learning from the liberal arts and learning from diversity?

Diversity Advances and Enriches the Liberal Arts

Learning about and from diversity increases the power of a liberal arts education (31). Similar to how different subjects in the liberal arts expose you to multiple perspectives, so do experiences with diversity. Diversity experiences expand your view of the world beyond the narrow-angle lens of your own culture (a monocultural perspective), equipping you with a wide-angle lens that enables you to view the world from a multicultural perspective. This multicultural perspective is consistent with one of the primary major goals of the liberal arts—to liberate (free) you from the tunnel vision of ethnocentrism (18).

Learning about others who differ from you also contributes to another major goal of the liberal arts: self-awareness. One of the most frequently cited outcomes of the liberal arts is to "know thyself" (81,279). Diversity contributes to this outcome by deepening self-awareness. When students around the country were interviewed about their diversity experiences in college, many of these students reported that these experiences enabled them to learn more about themselves. Some said that their interactions with students from different races and ethnic groups produced "unexpected" or "jarring" self-insights (180).

Lastly, diversity embodies the principles of a democratic nation and reinforces the original purpose of the liberal arts as a preserver of democracy (83, 128). The United States is a country built on the founding principle of equal rights and freedom of opportunity for all its citizens, including the immigrants from diverse countries and cultures who migrated to its shores. Prejudice and discrimination divide citizens and dislodge the cornerstone of democracy. When the rights or freedoms of any group of citizens in a democratic nation are undermined by prejudice and discrimination, the rights or freedoms of all its citizens are threatened. Given that diversity in America is growing, our nation's future stability and prosperity will require effective development and deployment of the talents of all its citizens, including those from historically diverse and disadvantaged backgrounds (8).

> "Injustice anywhere is a threat to justice everywhere."
>
> —Martin Luther King Jr., "Letter from the Birmingham Jail"

KEY POINT: Diversity and democracy go hand-in-hand; by valuing the former, we preserve the latter.

The original ideal of the liberal arts was to liberate people to participate in a democracy; in reality, not all people were included in the process. The "free men" who first devised and studied the liberal arts in Greece were aristocrats; they were privileged to have the position and time to study the liberal arts, and their opportunity to acquire greater knowledge further distanced them from enslaved serfs and

FIGURE 4.1

Liberal arts and diversity provide two key pillars of support for democracy.

peasants. Similarly, the liberal arts for democracy espoused by the founding fathers of the United States did not include enslaved African Americans, nor did it include American women who were denied the right to vote and other rights that were granted to white, male citizens. When members of minority and disadvantaged groups are denied the opportunity to influence public policies and societal practices, they are left with a sense of political helplessness and lose faith in the democratic system of government (226).

Fortunately, the modern version of the liberal arts embraces the view that all citizens have the right to a college education, which promotes equal opportunity and preserves democracy (80). This ideal can only be achieved if diversity is embraced and included as an integral element of the liberal arts. A core component of a comprehensive liberal arts curriculum is inclusiveness; it's a curriculum that includes and respects diverse people and cultures (189). This is why most American colleges and universities have added diversity as a core component of their general education curriculum (275).

"The Constitution of the United States knows no distinction between citizens on account of color."

—Frederick Douglass, abolitionist, author, advocate for equal rights for all people, and former slave

"A well-functioning democracy requires not only that differing views be heard and discussed but that decisions be made with an appreciation for those differences."

—Robert Shoenberg, Senior Fellow, Association of American Colleges and Universities

> "I want to study Asian history and women's history. I'm tired of studying about White people and men."
>
> —Overheard comment made by a female high school student to a friend at a coffee shop in California

> "A national culture or school curriculum that does not reflect the voices, struggles, hopes, and dreams of its many people is neither democratic nor cohesive."
>
> —National Council for the Social Sciences

When students see their ethnic identities represented in the curriculum, they see their cultural history is valued, which serves to promote their sense of political efficacy and their belief that participation in their nation's governance will make a difference for them (34).

When diversity is interwoven into the liberal arts curriculum, historical events are understood more completely and deeply because they're viewed through multiple cultural lenses (22). For instance, a complete understanding of American history must include awareness of the Indian Removal Act in 1830 that forced Native Americans to leave their reservations and move west, as well as the forced internment of Japanese Americans during World War II. Failure to include such events is not only insensitive to these minority groups, it also results in an incomplete and inaccurate understanding of American history.

Integrating diversity into the liberal arts enables all students to appreciate the common themes that unite humans (humanity) and cultural variations on those themes (diversity). This coalescence of unity and diversity creates a sense of community among a diverse student body (40). As we look to learn from diversity, we shouldn't overlook the unity that transcends our differences. Focusing exclusively on group differences without paying attention to the underlying themes that unite us can actually divide us. In fact, some studies show that when diversity education focuses on differences alone, minority groups are more likely to experience a stronger sense of separation and isolation (264).

KEY POINT

When the liberal arts and diversity are studied in tandem, you're able to dig below the surface of human differences and detect the shared roots from which these differences grow. Although groups of humans have different cultural backgrounds, these cultural differences are cultivated from the same soil—the common ground of humanity.

Diversity Expands and Enriches the Multiple Perspectives Developed by the Liberal Arts

As mentioned in Chapter 1, the liberal arts broaden your perspective to include other people, places, and times. The following sections of this chapter identify how diversity enriches and extends this broadening experience by exposing you to a variety of sub-perspectives embedded within each of the social–spatial and chronological perspectives developed by the liberal arts.

Diversity and the Perspective of Self

Interacting with people from diverse backgrounds increases self-knowledge and self-awareness by enabling you to compare your life experiences with others whose experiences may differ sharply from your own. When you step outside yourself to contrast your background with others from different backgrounds, you move beyond egocentrism and acquire a *comparative perspective*—a reference point that positions you to see how your particular cultural background has shaped the person you are today.

"It is difficult to see the picture when you are inside the frame."

—An old saying (author unknown)

A comparative perspective also enables us to learn how our cultural background has advantaged or disadvantaged us. For instance, learning about cross-cultural differences in education makes us aware of the limited opportunities people in other countries have to attend college and how advantaged we are in America—where a college education is available to everyone—regardless of their race, gender, age, or prior academic history.

| KEY POINT | The more you learn from cultures that differ from your own, the more you learn about yourself. |

Diversity and the Perspective of Family

To fully appreciate the concept of family is to appreciate the variety of ways in which families are formed. Family diversity includes differences in the number of parents present, number of children and extended family members living at home, racial makeup of family members, number of wage earners in the family, and the sexual orientation of the family's partners. Following are some of the diverse forms of families found in society today.

- Nuclear families: contain two spouses and one or more children
- Extended families: include members who are related to the nuclear family (e.g., grandparents, uncles, aunts, or adult children)
- Families with or without children
- Single-parent families: include one parent and one or more children
- Patriarchal families: the father is the major authority figure and decision maker
- Matriarchal families: the mother is the major authority figure and decision maker
- Multiethnic or multiracial families: include family members from more than one race or ethnic group
- Stepfamilies: one or both parents are not biological parents of the children
- Blended families: contain two or more siblings who are not related biologically, but who have become members of the same family through remarriage of one of their biological parents
- Single-income families: include only one wage-earner
- Families with adopted children
- Families with children whose parents are unmarried
- Families in which the partners are gay

As this list demonstrates, gaining a complete and accurate perspective of the American family requires taking multiple sub-perspectives and includes awareness of diverse familial arrangements.

PAUSE FOR THOUGHT

Which of the above family arrangements most closely corresponds to the one in which you were raised? In what way(s) do you think your family structure affected your development and the person you are today?

Author Experience—Barack Obama, forty-fourth president of the United States

As a child of a black man and a white woman, someone who was born in the racial melting pot of Hawaii, with a sister who's half Indonesian but who's usually mistaken for Mexican or Puerto Rican, and a brother-in-law and niece of Chinese descent, with some blood relatives who resemble Margaret Thatcher and others who could pass for Bernie Mac, family get-togethers over Christmas take on the appearance of a U.N. General Assembly meeting. I've never had the option of restricting my loyalties on the basis of race, or measuring my worth on the basis of tribe (224).

Diversity and the Perspective of Community

A comprehensive perspective of community requires appreciation of the diversity of communities that comprise society and influence human development. For instance, schools in our local communities play a major role in a person's educational development. Unfortunately, however, all schools are not created equal. Schools differ widely in terms of their resources, their facilities, and the racial and ethnic makeup of their student body.

America has a highly decentralized system of education, with more than 15,000 local school districts making their own decisions about instructional policies, programs, and practices. Decentralization does allow different schools the freedom to be responsive to the unique needs of their local community. However, a negative consequence of decentralization is that it has resulted in wide disparities in the quality of education experienced by children and adolescents in different school districts. Since schools are funded by local property taxes, the amount of fiscal resources available to schools in different communities varies considerably depending on the wealth of people living in the local community where the school is located. The wealthier the surrounding community, the more tax dollars are available to support its local schools. Thus, schools located in poorer communities typically have fewer educational resources and poorer physical facilities. For example, in 2005, school districts in communities serving the highest concentration of poor students received an average of $938 less per-pupil funding than districts serving students with the lowest poverty rates, and school districts serving the highest concentration of minority-group students received an average of $877 less per-student funding than districts serving the lowest concentration of students from minority groups (273).

> "You can easily judge the character of a man by how he treats those who can do nothing for him."
>
> —Jonathan Wolfgang von Goethe, influential nineteenth-century German writer and politician

A major goal of the liberal arts is to develop citizens of character. People with civic character are model community members who are respectful of and sensitive to the rights and needs of fellow citizens living in different communities. They also engage themselves in diverse communities, gaining experience with different groups of people by participating in community programs, volunteer service, and civic leadership. "Liberally educated people understand that they belong to a community whose prosperity and well-being are crucial to their own, and they help that community flourish by making the success of others possible" (80). Employers of college graduates feel the same way: National surveys indicate that more than 70 percent of employers agree that it's important for their employees to "show interest in giving back to the communities in which our company or organization is located or those that it serves" and 86 percent agree that "all students should have direct learning experiences working with others to solve problems important in their communities" (136).

Diversity and the Perspective of Society

Gaining a comprehensive societal perspective requires awareness that our society is now more ethnically and racially diverse than at any other time in history, and it will continue to grow more diverse throughout the twenty-first century (277). In 1995, 75 percent of America's population was white; by 2050, it will be 54 percent (281, 282). Minorities now account for 36.6 percent of the total population—an all-time high; in 2011, for the first time in U.S. history, racial and ethnic minorities made up more than half (50.4 percent) of all children born in America (218).

These demographic changes have created a multicultural society in which the ability to understand, relate to, and learn from people of diverse racial and ethnic backgrounds is essential for success in the twenty-first century (206, 264). Experiencing a liberal arts education infused with diversity will strengthen your ability to empathize with and relate to members of society whose cultural experiences differ from your own.

Diversity and the National Perspective

To appreciate America is to appreciate diversity. America has a long and unique history of accepting and assimilating people from different countries and cultures; diversity is a distinctive characteristic of our national identity. Immigrants from a wide variety of countries and cultures have built the foundation of this country—literally, because they have always done and continue to do the hardest physical labor for the least amount of pay. Lest we forget, the United States is a nation that was founded and developed by members of diverse immigrant groups, many of whom came to America's shores with the hope of escaping the prejudice and discrimination they faced in their native countries. They came to America with the dream of gaining personal freedom and attaining the opportunity to build a better life for themselves and their families (178).

The "American dream" is still being pursued by recent immigrants to the United States. In 2012, there were more than 40 million people born in different countries living in America, the highest total ever (126), and at least one of four speaks a language at home other than English (116).

> "The United States is a different kind of nation. Many Americans are immigrants or children of immigrants, are of varied races, adhere to different religions, and have richly diverse cultural backgrounds. What makes us Americans is our common set of values and a shared commitment to the political institutions that preserve them."
>
> —David Boren, president, University of Oklahoma and longest-serving chairman of the U.S. Senate Intelligence Committee

> **PAUSE FOR THOUGHT**
>
> Despite being a country that was originally and continues to be a home for immigrants from diverse nations, what common beliefs, attitudes, or values do you think all Americans share?

Diversity and the International Perspective

To take an international perspective is to appreciate the diversity of humankind. If it were possible to reduce the world's population to a village of precisely 100 people, with all existing human ratios remaining about the same, the demographics of this world village would look something like this:

61 would be Asians, 13 would be Africans, 12 would be Europeans, 9 would be Latin Americans, and 5 would be North Americans (citizens of the United States and Canada)
50 would be male, 50 would be female
75 would be non-white; 25 would be white
67 would be non-Christian; 33 would be Christian
80 would live in substandard housing
16 would be unable to read or write
50 would be malnourished and 1 dying of starvation
33 would be without access to a safe water supply
39 would lack access to modern sanitation
24 would have no electricity (and of the 76 who have electricity, most would only use it for light at night)
8 people would have access to the Internet
1 would have a college education
1 would have HIV
2 would be near birth; 1 near death
5 would control 32 percent of the entire world's wealth; all 5 would be U.S. citizens

Humanity, Diversity, and the Liberal Arts: Foundation of a College Education

48 would live on less than $2 a day
20 would live on less than $1 a day (102)

In this world village, English would not be the most common language spoken; it would be third, following Chinese and Spanish (179).

The need for American college students to develop an international perspective is highlighted by a study conducted by an anthropologist who went "undercover" to pose as a student in a university residence hall. She found that the biggest complaint international students had about American students was their lack of knowledge of other countries and the misconceptions they held about people from different nations (205). When you take the time to learn about other countries and the cultures of people who inhabit them, you move beyond being just a citizen of your own nation, you become *cosmopolitan*—a citizen of the world.

Diversity and the Global Perspective

A global perspective includes human diversity, but extends beyond it to embrace *biodiversity*—variations in all life forms inhabiting planet Earth. Biodiversity is sustained by *ecosystem* diversity—when different biological, climatic, geological, and chemical ingredients in the environmental system combine to maintain the life of the planet's plants and animals (221). Thus, the contemporary issue of environmental sustainability is actually a diversity issue; sustaining biodiversity depends on sustaining the diversity of the ecosystem. The worldwide significance of this issue is highlighted by the fact that the United Nations declared 2010 as the "International Year of Biodiversity" (IYB) to raise global awareness that preserving biodiversity requires the collective environmental efforts of all nations (280).

Diversity and the Universe (Cosmos)

Diversity not only characterizes humanity and all life forms inhabiting the planet, it also characterizes the universe. Just as we should guard against ethnocentrism and anthropocentrism, we should guard against *geocentricism*—viewing our planet as the center of the uni-

> "The sun, with all those planets revolving around it and dependent on it, can still ripen a bunch of grapes as if it had nothing else in the universe to do."
>
> —Galileo Galilei

verse. All heavenly bodies do not revolve around our plant; instead, our earth revolves around them. The sun doesn't rise in the east and set in the west; it's our planet that rotates around the sun to create our earthly experiences of day and night.

In summary, all the broadening social–spatial perspectives of the liberal arts cannot be fully understood without appreciating the diversity embedded within each of them. Understanding the broadening perspectives of the liberal arts along with the diverse sub-perspectives that comprise them serve to liberate or "de-center" us from narrow, self-centered perspectives—such as those summarized in **Box 4.1**.

BOX 4.1

Narrow Viewpoints Combated by the Broadening Perspectives of the Liberal Arts and Diversity

1. **Egocentrism**—narrowly focusing on one's personal needs while failing to appreciate the needs and perspectives of other people in other places.
2. **Parochialism** (a.k.a. **Provincialism**)—narrow-mindedness and unwillingness to expand one's viewpoints beyond a local or regional perspective.
3. **Ethnocentrism**—belief that the customs and values of one's own culture are superior to all other cultures.
4. **Nationalism**—belief that the interests, needs, or wants of one's own nation should be placed ahead of all other nations.
5. **Anthropocentrism**—belief that human needs or wants take precedence over all other life forms and planetary resources.
6. **Geocentrism**—viewing planet Earth as the center of the universe.

Diversity and the Chronological Perspective

The chronological perspective developed by the liberal arts becomes comprehensive and complete when it includes a multicultural perspective on the dimension of time. Cross-cultural studies indicate that Western cultures (e.g., United States and Canada) tend to view time from a "monochronic" perspective, focusing primarily on the present (the "here and now") and seeing chronological events as a series of successive episodes rather than as an evolving chain of interconnected events. In contrast, Eastern cultures (e.g., China and India) are more likely to take a "polychromic" perspective, whereby time is less likely to be viewed in terms of separate, discrete segments, but more as a continuum in which the three dimensions of time (past, present, future) merge together to form a continuous flow of interdependent experiences (176, 222). A more integrated and comprehensive understanding of the historical, contemporary, and futuristic perspectives developed by the liberal arts is attained when the dimension of time is viewed through the lenses of both Western and Eastern cultures.

Diversity and the Historical Perspective

Incorporating diversity into our historical perspective serves to elevate our awareness of how different groups of people have struggled to gain personal freedom, human rights, and social justice, and how these past events continue to influence how diverse groups are treated today. For instance, a historical perspective leads to a clearer understanding of current-day concepts of race and racism. Historically, the word "race" did not even exist until Americans introduced the term in the eighteenth and nineteenth centuries. At that point in American history, the cotton industry was booming, which created demand for more land and a larger labor force. To meet these needs, wealthy white Americans devised and disseminated the idea of a privileged "white race" to justify taking land from Native Americans for the purpose of developing more plantations and using African Americans as slaves to build a larger labor force (33, 109). Prior to that point in time, the term "race" was not used anywhere else in the world. English settlers created the phrase "white race" to distinguish themselves from Native Americans and African Americans whom they deemed to be "uncivilized," "savages," or "subhuman."

> "We cannot expect that a nation which has lost its memory will keep its vision. We cannot hope that forgetting our past will enhance our focus on the future."
>
> —Bruce Cole, former chair of the National Endowment for the Humanities

Thus, white privilege was gained at the expense of oppressing groups deemed to be "non-white" and provided the historical roots of contemporary racism. American immigrants who initially defined themselves as German, Irish, or Italian slowly began to refer to themselves as "white" as they began to move up to higher levels of socioeconomic and political status (103).

Another element of human diversity that needs to be incorporated into our historical perspective is *generational* diversity. Humans are diverse with respect to the historical time period in which they grew up. The term "generation" refers to a cohort (group) of individuals born during the same period in history whose attitudes, values, and habits have been shaped by events that took place in the world during their formative years of development. Since each generation experiences different historical events, people growing up in different generations are likely to develop different attitudes and beliefs. Contained in **Box 4.2** is a brief summary of different generations, the key historical events they experienced, and the personal characteristics commonly associated with each generational group (124).

BOX 4.2

Generational Diversity

- **The Traditional Generation (a.k.a. "Silent Generation")** (born 1922–1945). This generation was influenced by events such as the Great Depression and World Wars I and II. Characteristics associated with people growing up at this time include loyalty, patriotism, respect for authority, and conservatism.
- **The Baby Boomer Generation** (born 1946–1964). This generation was influenced by events such as the Vietnam War, Watergate, and the human rights movement. Characteristics associated with people growing up at this time include idealism, emphasis on self-fulfillment, and concern for social justice and equal rights.

- **Generation X** (born 1965–1980). This generation was influenced by *Sesame Street*, the creation of MTV, AIDS, and soaring divorce rates. They were the first "latchkey children"—youngsters who used their own key to let themselves into their home after school—because their mother (or single mother) was working outside the home. Characteristics associated with people growing up at this time include self-reliance, resourcefulness, and ability to adapt to change.
- **Generation Y** (a.k.a. "Millennials") (born 1981–2002). This generation was influenced by the September 11, 2001, terrorist attack on the United States, the shooting of students at Columbine High School, and the collapse of the Enron Corporation. Characteristics associated with people growing up at this time include a preference for working and playing in groups, familiarity with technology, and willingness to engage in volunteer service in their community (the "civic generation"). This is also the most ethnically diverse generation, which may explain why they're more open to diversity than previous generations and more likely to view it as a positive experience.
- **Generation Z** (a.k.a. "The iGeneration") (born 1994–present). This generation includes the latter half of Generation Y. They grew up during the wars in Afghanistan and Iraq and are familiar with the unpredictability of safety in public spaces; consequently, they are likely to have a higher degree of mistrust in existing political systems. During their formative years, the World Wide Web was in place, so they're quite comfortable with and rely heavily on the Internet, Wikipedia, Google, Twitter, MySpace, Facebook, Instant Messaging, imageboards and YouTube. They expect immediate gratification through technology and accept the lack of privacy associated with social networking. For these reasons, they're also referred to as the "digital generation."

"You guys [in the media] have to get used to it. This is a new day and age, and for my generation that's a very common word. It's like saying 'bro'. That's how we address our friends. That's how we talk."

—Matt Barnes, 33-year-old, biracial professional basketball player, explaining to reporters after being fined for using the word "niggas" in a tweet

PAUSE FOR THOUGHT

Look back at the characteristics associated with your generation. Which of these characteristics accurately reflect your personal characteristics and those of your closest friends? Which do not?

Diversity and the Contemporary Perspective

When diversity is viewed from a contemporary perspective, it's clear that significant progress has been made with respect to social justice and human equality. For instance, the ethnic and racial diversity of students attending college in America is now at an all-time high. In 1960, whites made up almost 95 percent of the total college population; in 2010, that percentage had decreased to 61.5 percent. Between 1976 and 2010, the percentage of ethnic minority students in higher education increased from 17 to 40 percent (209).

This rise in ethnic and racial diversity on American campuses today is particularly noteworthy when viewed in light of the historical treatment of minority groups in the United States. In the early nineteenth century, education was not a right, but a privilege available only to those who could afford to attend private schools, mainly Protestants of European descent. Later, immigrants from other cultural backgrounds began migrating to the United States and public education became mandatory; its goal was to "Americanize" these new immigrants and obliterate their own cultural identities in the process (184). Members of certain minority groups were left out of the educational process altogether or were forced to be educated in racially segregated settings. Americans of color were taught in separate, segregated schools that were typically inferior in terms of educational resources and facilities. It was not until the groundbreaking Supreme Court ruling in *Brown vs. Board of Education* (May 17, 1954) that the face of education was changed for people of color. On that day, the U.S. Su-

> "Of all the civil rights for which the world has struggled and fought for 5,000 years, the right to learn is undoubtedly the most fundamental."
>
> —W.E.B. Dubois, African American sociologist, historian, and civil rights activist

preme Court ruled that "separate educational facilities are inherently unequal." This decision made it illegal for Kansas and twenty other states to deliver education in segregated classrooms.

Author Experience—Aaron Thompson

My mother was a direct descendent of slaves and moved with her parents from the Deep South at the age of seventeen. My father lived in an all-black coal mining camp in Kentucky, into which my mother and her family moved in 1938. My father remained illiterate because he was not allowed to attend public schools in eastern Kentucky.

In the early 1960s, I was integrated into the white public schools along with my brother and sister. Physical violence and constant verbal harassment caused many other blacks to quit school at an early age and opt for jobs in the coal mines. But my father remained constant in his advice to me: "It doesn't matter if they call you n_____; don't you ever let them beat you by walking out on your education." He'd say to me, "Son, you will have opportunities that I never had. Many people, white and black alike, will tell you that you are no good and that education can never help you. Don't listen to them because soon they will not be able to keep you from getting an education like they did me. Just remember, when you do get that education, you'll never have to go in those coal mines and have them break your back. You can choose what you want to do, and then you can be a free man."

Being poor, black, and Appalachian did not offer me great odds for success, but constant reminders from my parents that I was a worthy person and that education was the key to my future freedom and happiness enabled me to beat the odds. My parents were not able to provide me with monetary wealth, but they did provide me with the gifts of self-worth, educational motivation, and aspiration for academic achievement.

"Knowledge is freedom . . . ignorance is slavery."

—Miles Davis, influential twentieth-centruy jazz trumpeter and musical innovator

In addition to growing more racially and ethnically diverse, American colleges have also grown more diverse with respect to *gender* and *age*. In 1955, only 25 percent of college students were female; by 2000, the percentage had jumped to almost 66 percent (243). From 1990 to 2009, the proportion of women enrolled in college increased at a rate that almost tripled the rate of males in the same age range (163).

Also increasing is the percentage of students 24 years of age or older attending college, jumping from 28 percent in 1970 to 44 percent today (69, 285). Over one-third of American students enrolled in college are over the age of 25 (66*)*. More so than any other time in American history, the diversity of students on American college campuses embodies the ideals of a liberal arts—to provide a liberating education for *all* Americans—regardless of their culture, color, creed, age, or gender (18).

> "The curriculum should help students understand the significant historical experiences of ethnic groups [and] the critical contemporary issues and social problems confronting each of them."
>
> —National Council for the Social Sciences

However, despite great progress in our nation's acceptance, appreciation, and education of different ethnic and racial groups, the United States remains a nation deeply divided with respect to culture, religion, and social class (50). Lingering consequences and residual "ripple effects" of earlier injustices continue to disadvantage certain groups of Americans today. For instance, the manner in which African Americans were exploited and stereotyped has left a long-standing mark on their current experiences. Black Americans continue to encounter prejudice and discrimination in a more subtle form—known as *institutional racism*—a less direct but still damaging form of racism that's deeply rooted in our society's organizational structures, policies, and practices. Institutional racism manifests itself in such practices as race-based discrimination in mortgage lending, housing, and bank loans. "Redlining"—a term coined in the late 1960s to describe the practice of marking a red line on a map to indicate an area where banks would not invest or lend money—still continues today. Many of these redlined areas are neighborhoods inhabited predominantly by African Americans (258). Additional studies show that compared to White patients, Black patients of the same socioeconomic status are less likely to receive equal medical treatment. For instance, they're less likely to receive breast cancer screening, follow-up visits after hospitalization for mental illness, and eye examinations if they have diabetes (253).

Similarly, despite the fact that women are now able to hold professional positions that were once reserved exclusively for men, females still experience inequities with respect to employment compensation. In 1963, women earned 59 cents for every dollar earned by men, which prompted President John F. Kennedy to sign the Equal Pay Act, making it illegal for employers to pay unequal wages to men and women who performed the same jobs. Still, in 2012, as it was ten years earlier, full-time, year-round female workers were paid 77 percent of what men were paid (7). Females with graduate degrees earn only slightly more than males with a high school diploma: $41,995 for women vs. $40,822 for men (251).

Wage gaps also continue to exist in many professional occupations. For example, females earn only a percentage of male salaries in the following professions:

- Physicians: 61%
- Property/real estate: 61%
- Sales: 63%
- Chief executives (CEOs): 69%
- Construction: 79%
- Computers and mathematics: 86% (59, 211)

These wage gaps exist even when women attain the same level of education as their male counterparts (7).

PAUSE FOR THOUGHT

Are females likely to be represented in equal numbers as males in the career field(s) you are considering? Why do you think this is the case?

Diversity and the Futuristic Perspective

America's racial and ethnic groups that have been called "minorities" will soon become the "new majority" (117). By 2050, the U.S. population is projected to be more than 30 percent Hispanic (up from 15 percent in 2008), 15 percent Black (up from 13 percent in 2008), 9.6 percent Asian (up from 5.3 percent in 2008), and 2 percent Native Americans (up from 1.6 percent in 2008). The Native Hawaiian and Pacific Islander population is also expected to more than double between 2008 and 2050. During the same timeframe, the percentage of white Americans will decline from 66 percent to 46 percent. As a result of these demographic trends, today's ethnic and racial minorities will constitute the majority of Americans by the middle of the twenty-first century (282). Thus, the future prosperity of the United States will depend on our nation's ability to appreciate and capitalize on its growing diversity, and must include the new majority of future Americans in the "American dream."

Diversity Magnifies the Benefits of Liberal Arts

In Chapter 2, the benefits of experiencing the liberal arts were catalogued and documented. When diversity is infused into the liberal arts, these benefits are multiplied. Described next are the ways in which diversity enriches and extends the benefits of the liberal arts.

Diversity Broadens Your Personal Interests and Builds Social Self-Confidence

"Variety is the spice of life."

–An old American proverb

"Viva la difference!" (Long live difference!)

—An old French saying

Learning about a wide range of subjects broadens your knowledge base and strengthens your social self-confidence (80, 195), and so do experiences with diversity. Enhancing your social versatility makes you a more interesting (and interested) person who's more likely to add to conversations and less likely to be left out of conversations or have the topic of conversation "go over your head" (261) (or outside your comfort zone). Research indicates that students who have more diversity experiences in college report higher levels of satisfaction with their college experience (19). Furthermore when you widen the range of people with whom you interact, you also gain greater ability to adapt to unfamiliar social situations, which serves to increase your intellectual self-confidence (67, 195).

Diversity Accelerates and Deepens Learning

Learning about different cultures and interacting with diverse groups of people adds to the variety of neural connections stored in our brain, which provides more varied routes or pathways through which to connect (learn) new ideas. Experiencing diversity also "stretches" the brain beyond its normal "comfort zone" because it must work harder to assimilate something that's different or unfamiliar. The only way we can learn something that's unfamiliar or very different is by making the extra mental effort to compare and contrast it to something we already know (3, 202). To make this mental "stretch," the brain must expend extra psychological energy; the expenditure of added mental energy creates neurological connections that are deeper and more durable. This explains why research consistently shows that we learn more from people who differ from us than we do from people similar to us (230, 232). Simply stated, humans learn more from diversity than they do from similarity or familiarity. In contrast, when we restrict the diversity of people with whom we interact (out of habit or prejudice), we limit the breadth and depth of our learning.

A large body of research also indicates that students learn more deeply when learning takes place in a *social* context that involves interpersonal *interaction* and *collaboration* (84, 86). As scholars put it, knowledge is "socially constructed"—it's built up through interpersonal interaction and dialogue (58). According to this *social constructivist* theory of human learning, our thinking consists largely of "internal" (mental) representations of conversations we have with other people (289). Thus, the better the quality and variety of our conversations, the better is the quality and complexity of our thinking. By interacting with and learn from culturally diverse people, the nature of our thinking becomes more diversified, nuanced, and complete.

A good example of how the quality of our thinking is strengthened by experiences with diversity is our discovery that a diet high in unsaturated fats (and low in saturated fats) is an effective strategy for reducing the risk of cardiovascular disease (9). This knowledge was gained by learning from the cultural experiences of Eskimos, whose extraordinarily low rate of cardiovascular disease has been traced to the natural oils they consume as part of their fish-rich diet; these oils contain a type of unsaturated fat that flushes out and washes away cholesterol-forming fats from the bloodstream (105, 162). Similarly, as a result of our studying the culture and practices of Indian Buddhists, we have learned meditation and yoga are effective, drug-free strategies for managing stress (39, 293).

KEY POINT

By interacting and collaborating with members of different cultural groups, we create a win-win situation: we learn from them and they learn from us.

Diversity Strengthens the Liberal Arts' Capacity to Promote Critical Thinking from Multiple Perspectives

Both multicultural and multidisciplinary experiences serve to liberate you from narrowness; each empowers you to view yourself and the world around you from a variety of perspectives. Just as exposure to a diversity of disciplines in the liberal arts curriculum opens your mind to multiple perspectives, so too does exposure to the diversity of human cultures. Experiencing diversity further expands the multiplicity of perspectives from which you can understand and solve problems.

> "The nation's future depends upon leaders trained through wide exposure to that robust exchange of ideas which discovers truth out of a multitude of tongues."
>
> —William J. Brennan, former Supreme Court justice

Research on college students indicates that their critical thinking skills develop most when "divergent views are aggressively sought" (123). Other studies show that students who experience high levels of exposure to different dimensions of diversity while in college, such as participating in multicultural courses and campus events and interacting with peers of different ethnic backgrounds, report the greatest gains in:

* **thinking *complexity*** —the ability to think about all parts and from all sides of an issue (17, 127);
* ***reflective* thinking**—the ability to think deeply about personal and global issues (166); and

Humanity, Diversity, and the Liberal Arts: Foundation of a College Education

* *critical* **thinking**—the ability to evaluate the validity of their own reasoning and the reasoning of others (233).

These findings are likely explained by the fact that when we operate within the safety of this cultural comfort zone, it requires minimal effort to understand and be understood by others; this puts the brain on cruise control or autopilot. In contrast, exposure to diverse people and multiple perspectives makes our thinking more effortful and tends to induce "cognitive dissonance"—a state of cognitive (mental) disequilibrium or imbalance, which "forces" our mind to focus on and deal with these multiple perspectives simultaneously (49, 123).

The multiple perspective-taking promoted by diversity also helps us become aware of our cultural "blind spots" and avoid two dangerous limitations of single-perspective thinking:

1. **Group polarization**—When like-minded people get together to discuss their views, their point of view becomes more extreme and they're more likely to take riskier courses of action (201, 295).
2. **Groupthink**—When like-minded people work together in the same group, they're less likely to challenge each other's thinking and more likely to overlook the flaws in their own thinking, which can lead them to erroneous choices and decisions (25, 151).

"When all men think alike, no one thinks very much."

—Walter Lippman, distinguished journalist and originator of the term "stereotype"

Group polarization and groupthink contributed to American doctors' erroneous conclusion that acupuncture, a long-used Chinese method of pain relief, was quackery; this retarded its eventual adoption in America as an effective alternative to pain-killing drugs (149).

KEY POINT

Associating exclusively with the same group of people not only limits you socially, it also limits you mentally.

PAUSE FOR THOUGHT

> Do you intentionally seek out ideas from others who have different cultural backgrounds than your own? If yes, why? If no, why not?

Experiencing divergent views and diverse perspectives encourages you to ask questions about why different viewpoints are held and increases your awareness of how your own cultural background shapes your perception or interpretation of events. It also helps you to critically evaluate the ideas you're exposed to in different subject areas and determine whether they're accurate, complete, or biased by the author's particular cultural perspective (23, 24). Be ready to ask yourself: "Whose voice is speaking and whose voice am I not hearing?" and "What cultural perspective (or bias) is the author or producer bringing to this book, website, or movie?" (122,123)

Diversity Stimulates Creative Thinking

Studies of creative people reveal they have a wide range interests and knowledge that cross disciplinary boundaries, enabling them to draw on ideas from multiple subject areas (21, 249). Similarly, cross-cultural knowledge and experiences enhance personal creativity (177, 186). Diversity further broadens the base of knowledge and range of thinking styles developed by the liberal arts, empowering us to think beyond the mental boundaries set by our prior cultural conditioning. When we have diverse perspectives at our disposal, we have more opportunities to shift perspectives and discover "multiple partial solutions" to problems (161). Furthermore, ideas acquired from diverse people and cultures can "cross-fertilize," giving birth to new ideas for tackling old problems (133). Research shows that when ideas are generated freely and exchanged openly in groups comprised of people from diverse backgrounds, powerful "cross-stimulation" effects can occur, whereby ideas from one group member trigger new ideas among other group members (55).

> **KEY POINT**
> By drawing on ideas generated by people from diverse backgrounds and bouncing your ideas off them, divergent (expansive) thinking is stimulated, which leads to synergy—multiplication of ideas, and serendipity—unexpected discoveries.

In contrast, when different cultural perspectives are neither sought nor valued, the variety of lenses available to us for viewing problems is reduced, which, in turn, reduces our capacity to think creatively. Ideas are less likely to diverge (go in different directions); instead, they're more likely to converge and merge into the same cultural channel—the one shared by the homogeneous group of people doing the thinking.

> **PAUSE FOR THOUGHT**
>
> How do you think your performance in your college major will be strengthened by your experience with:
> 1. Liberal arts?
> 2. Diversity?

Diversity Enhances Career Preparation and Career Success

Whatever line of work you decide to pursue, you're likely to find yourself working with employers, co-workers, customers, and clients from diverse cultural backgrounds. America's workforce is now more diverse than at any other time in the nation's history and it will grow

"What I look for in musicians is generosity. There is so much to learn from each other and about each other's culture. Great creativity begins with tolerance."

—Yo-Yo Ma, French-born, Chinese American virtuoso cellist, composer, and winner of multiple Grammy Awards

"When the only tool you have is a hammer, you tend to see every problem as a nail."

—Abraham Maslow, humanistic psychologist, best known for his self-actualization theory of human motivation

> "The benefits that accrue to college students who are exposed to racial and ethnic diversity during their education carry over in the work environment. The improved ability to think critically, to understand issues from different points of view, and to collaborate harmoniously with co-workers from a range of cultural backgrounds all enhance a graduate's ability to contribute to his or her company's growth and productivity."
>
> —Business/Higher Education Forum

ever more diverse throughout the twenty-first century. The proportion of America's working-age population comprised of workers from minority ethnic and racial groups is expected to jump to 55 percent in 2050 (282).

National surveys reveal that policymakers, business leaders, and employers seek college graduates who are more than just "aware" of or "tolerant" of diversity. They want graduates who have actual *experience* with diversity (98) and are able to collaborate with diverse co-workers, clients, and customers (16, 136). Over 90 percent of employees agree that all students should have experiences in college that teach them how to solve problems with people whose views are different from their own (136).

The results of employer surveys are reinforced by findings from surveys of American voters—the overwhelming majority of whom agree that diversity education helps students learn practical skills essential for success in today's work world—such as communication, teamwork, and problem solving. Almost one-half of surveyed voters also think that the American school system should "put more emphasis on teaching students about others' cultures, backgrounds and lifestyles" (215). Thus, both employers and the American public agree that diversity education is *career preparation*.

> "Only a well-educated, diverse work force, comprised of people who have learned to work productively and creatively with individuals from a multitude of races and ethnic, religious, and cultural backgrounds, can maintain America's competitiveness in the increasingly diverse and interconnected world economy."
>
> —Spokesman for General Motors Corporation (68)

The current "global economy" also requires skills relating to international diversity. The world of work today is characterized by economic interdependence among nations, international trading (imports/exports), multinational corporations, international travel, and almost instantaneous worldwide communication—due to rapid advances in the World Wide Web (95, 111). Even smaller companies and corporate organizations have become increasingly international in nature (51). As a result, employers in all sectors of the economy now seek job candidates who possess the following skills and attributes: sensitivity to human differences, ability to understand and relate to people from different cultural backgrounds, international knowledge, and ability to communicate in a second language (108, 207, 225, 136).

As a result of these domestic and international trends, *intercultural competence* has become an essential, transferable skill needed for success in the twenty-first century (275). Intercultural competence may be defined as the ability to appreciate and learn from human differences and to interact effectively with people from diverse cultural backgrounds. It includes "knowledge of cultures and cultural practices (one's own and others), complex cognitive skills for decision making in intercultural contexts, social skills to function effectively in diverse groups and personal attributes that include flexibility and openness to new ideas" (290).

"Technology and advanced communications have transformed the world into a global community, with business colleagues and competitors as likely to live in India as in Indianapolis. In this environment, people need a deeper understanding of the thinking, motivations, and actions of different cultures, countries and regions."

—The Partnership for 21st Century Skills

PAUSE FOR THOUGHT

What intercultural skills or competencies do you already possess?

What intercultural skills or competencies do you need to develop?

Internet Resources

For additional information related to the ideas discussed in this chapter, see the following websites:

"Does diversity make a difference?":
    http://www.aaup.org/NR/rdonlyres/97003B7B-055F-4318-B14A-5336321FB742/0/DIVREP.PDF

"Benefits of diversity":
    https://www.uwosh.edu/stuaff/images/BenefitsOfDiversity.pdf

"Research reveals the benefits of diversity for all students":
    http://www.diversityweb.org/digest/w97/research.html

"Benefits of diverse communities":
    http://aricherlife.org/benefits.html

"Top ten economic facts about benefits of diversity in the workplace":
    http://www.americanprogress.org/issues/labor/news/2012/07/12/11900/the-top-10-economic-facts-of-diversity-in-the-workplace/

Chapter Summary and Highlights

Learning about and from diversity increases the power of the liberal arts. Consistent with the broadening perspectives developed by the liberal arts, diversity expands your view of the world beyond the narrow-angle lens of your own culture (a monocultural perspective) and liberates you from the tunnel vision of ethnocentrism. Just as exposure to different disciplines in the liberal arts curriculum opens your mind to multiple perspectives, so too does exposure to the diversity of human cultures. By interacting with and learning from culturally diverse people, the nature of your thinking becomes more diversified, nuanced, and complete.

Learning about and from diversity also contributes to another major goal of the liberal arts: to "know thyself" (i.e., self-awareness). When students around the country were interviewed about their diversity experiences in college, many reported that these experiences enabled them to learn more about themselves.

A liberal arts curriculum should be an inclusive curriculum—that is, it should include and respect diverse people and cultures. This is why most American colleges and universities have added diversity as a core component of general education. When diversity is interwoven into the general education curriculum, a college education becomes more accurate and complete because events and ideas are not viewed through a single cultural lens. Integrating diversity into the liberal arts enables all students to appreciate the common themes that unite humans (humanity) as well as the cultural variations on those themes (diversity). This coalescence of unity and diversity creates a sense of community among a diverse student body.

Diversity infused into general education magnifies the benefits of the liberal arts; it enriches and extends the social–spatial and chronological perspectives by exposing you to a variety of sub-perspectives embedded within each of the liberal arts. Learning about a wide range of subject broadens your knowledge base and strengthens your social self-confidence; so do experiences with diversity. Diversity enhances your social versatility, making you a more interesting (and interested) person who's more likely to add to conversations and less likely to be left out of conversations or have the topic of conversation go over your head.

Diversity also accelerates and deepens learning by adding to the variety of neural connections stored in our brain, providing more varied routes or pathways through which to connect (learn) new ideas. Research consistently shows that we learn more from people who differ from us than we do from people similar to us. These results are likely due to the fact that experiencing diversity "stretches" the brain beyond its normal "comfort zone," making it work harder to assimilate something that's different or unfamiliar. The brain must expend extra psychological energy to make this mental stretch, and this expenditure of added mental energy results in the creation of neurological connections that are deeper and more durable. In addition, diversity stimulates creative thinking. By drawing on ideas generated by people from diverse backgrounds and bouncing your ideas off them, divergent (expansive) thinking is stimulated, which leads to synergy (multiplication of ideas) and serendipity (unexpected discoveries).

Lastly, diversity enhances career reparation and career success. America's workforce is now more diverse than at any other time in the nation's history and it will grow ever more diverse throughout the twenty-first century. National surveys reveal that policymakers, business leaders, and employers seek college graduates who are more than just "aware" of or "tolerant" of diversity. They want graduates who have actual experience with diversity and are able to collaborate with diverse co-workers, clients, and customers. Furthermore, the current "global economy" demands skills relating to international diversity. As a result of these domestic and international trends, *intercultural competence*—the ability to appreciate and learn from human differences and to interact effectively with people from diverse cultural backgrounds—has become another transferable liberal-arts skill needed for success in the twenty-first century.

Questions and Final Reflections

1. Look back at the six narrow "centric" viewpoints listed in Box 4.1. For each viewpoint, provide an example that illustrates or demonstrates it.

2. Think of a culture or community you have visited or had contact with that differs significantly from your own.
   (a) What made it different?
   (b) What would you say are the major advantages and disadvantages of living in that culture or community? Why?

3. In light of the ideas discussed in this chapter, how would you interpret or react to the following quotes?
   (a) "The more eyes, different eyes, we can use to observe one thing, the more complete will our concept of this thing, our objectivity, be."
   —Friedrich Nietzsche, German philosopher
   (b) "Most people today think of college primarily as a stepping stone to well-paid careers but not as a vital means for achieving better government or stronger communities."
   —Derek Bok, president emeritus and research professor, Harvard University
   (c) "When all men think alike, no one thinks very much."
   —Walter Lippman, distinguished journalist and political commentator

4. From your perspective, what historical event and historical figure have had the most positive influence on America?

   Do you think your answer to this question was influenced by your cultural background?
   If yes, why? If no, why not?

5. Identify three issues or topics that you think are important to all human beings regardless of their particular cultural background. Explain why you think each of these issues or topics transcends cultural differences.

Tying It All Together:
Developing a Plan for Making the Most of the Liberal Arts and Diversity

PAUSE FOR THOUGHT

If you were to develop a long-range educational plan for college, what would you include as its key components?

Compared to high school, college provides you with a broader range of courses to choose from and more control over the specific courses you take and when you take them. With respect to the liberal arts curriculum, you will have decision-making opportunities about what particular courses you take to fulfill general education requirements.

The first step in this decision-making process is to become familiar with the general education requirements on your campus. As mentioned in the first chapter of this book, you're likely to find these requirements organized into general divisions of knowledge (e.g., Humanities, Fine Arts, Natural Sciences, and Behavioral and Social Sciences). Within these divisions, specific courses fulfill general education requirement(s) for that particular division. In some cases, you will have no choice about the courses you must take to fulfill a general education requirement, but more likely than not, your campus will allow you some choice about what courses you can take to fulfill requirements in each of the major divisions of the liberal arts. For example, you may have a general education requirement in social or behavioral sciences that requires you to take two courses in this division, but you'll be allowed to choose those two courses from a menu of courses in the field—such as anthropology, economics, political science, psychology, or sociology.

With some careful forethought, you can develop a plan for general education that maximizes the power of the liberal arts and the return on your investment in a college education. Described next are specific strategies for developing such a plan.

Developing a General Education Plan for Making the Most of the Liberal Arts

Enroll in courses that expose you to each of the broadening social–spatial and chronological perspectives developed by the liberal arts. You can design a general education plan that intentionally develops each of the "liberating" perspectives of a liberal arts education. (Chapter 5 Exercise in the Appendix supplies a planning template you can use as of plan for ensuring that the multiple perspectives of the liberal arts are included in your general education experience.) If you're unable to enroll in courses that specifically address each of these broadening perspectives of the liberal arts, then you can still make a conscious attempt to apply the broadening social–spatial, chronological, and holistic (whole-self) perspectives to any course you take. These perspectives, described in Chapter 1, may be used as checklists to ensure that you are taking a comprehensive, multiple perspective view of any topic or issue you're studying.

When creating your plan, don't forget that general education also includes co-curricular learning experiences outside the classroom (e.g., leadership and volunteer experiences) designed to promote holistic development—that is, development of the whole person. Your Student Handbook probably represents the best source for information about co-curricular experiences offered on your campus. (See Chapter 5 Exercise in the Appendix for a planning template you can use to ensure that the key dimensions of holistic development are included in your general education experience.)

If you are uncertain about a college major or minor, use your general education requirements to test your interests and talents in fields that you might choose as a major or minor. If you're considering a subject as a possible major, take a general education course in that field to test your interest in it and your aptitude for it. This will allow you to explore your interest and ability in the subject, and at the same time, enable you to fulfill a general education requirement for graduation.

As a first-year student, it may be unrealistic for you to make a final decision about a college major before you've had at least some experience with the academic fields that comprise the college curriculum. One key benefit of experiencing the liberal arts at the start of your college career is that you're exposed to a wide variety of subjects and develop the critical thinking skills needed to make well-informed choices, including your choice of a college major.

"Your work is to discover your work and then with all your heart to give yourself to it."

–Buddha, a.k.a., Hindu Prince Gautama Siddharta (563–483 BC), founder of Buddhism

PAUSE FOR THOUGHT

If you have already decided on a college major, or if you're strongly considering one, what (or who) led you to this choice?

Choose elective courses with an eye toward strengthening your liberal arts education. Electives are courses that you elect or choose to take; they are not required for general education or your college major, but they count toward the total number of college credits needed for a baccalaureate (bachelor's) degree. Electives give you the freedom to choose any course listed in your college catalog. The collection of electives you choose to take over the course of your college experience will leave you with a final transcript that's different than any other college graduate.

The following suggestions are offered as guidelines for using your free electives in ways that will distinguish your college transcript and magnify the power of the liberal arts component of your college education.

1. Use electives to take courses that develop *transferable and enduring* skills you can use across the curriculum and throughout life.

You can take courses in the liberal arts not only to fulfill general education requirements, but also as electives to further develop your repertoire of lifelong-learning skills. For instance, even if you have completed the minimum number of writing courses to fulfill the general education requirement for English composition, you can further develop and diversify your writing skills by taking elective courses in writing (e.g., creative writing). In a study of college alumni who were surveyed ten years after graduation and asked about the importance of different skills to their current work responsibilities, more than 90 percent of them ranked "need to write effectively" as a skill that they considered to be of "great importance" to their current work (180).

The same is true for oral communication. Lest we forget, oral communication was included as a core subject in the original liberal arts curriculum designed by the ancient Greeks. It continues to be relevant for personal and professional success in the twenty-first century; research repeatedly shows that employers place high value on oral communication skills, ranking them among the top characteristics they seek in prospective employees (1, 206, 75, 134). Consider using some of your electives on courses that develop your public speaking skills (e.g., debate or forensics), particularly if your college or university does not require a course in public speaking as part of its general education curriculum.

2. If your campus offers them, take elective interdisciplinary courses.

The college curriculum is composed of academic disciplines or divisions of knowledge that represent separate, specialized fields of study. Interdisciplinary courses are intentionally designed to break down barriers between disciplines by integrating two or more fields of study. Such courses provide you with a more complete and balanced understanding of any topic or issue. For example, psychobiology is an interdisciplinary course that integrates the fields of psychology (focus on the mind) and biology (focus on the body), combining the two in a way that enables you to understand how the mind influences the body and vice versa.

Howard Gardner, internationally acclaimed researcher and author, points out that successful workers and leaders of the future will not only need "disciplined" minds that have mastered a specific body of knowledge, but also "synthesizing" minds that can integrate different bodies of knowledge (115). The ability to build conceptual bridges across isolated islands of knowledge requires higher-level interdisciplinary thinking. Studies show that when the brain works to integrate separate subjects, more elaborate connective pathways are established, which results in learning that's more deeply rooted and more durable (294).

Furthermore, making connections between different subjects is a mentally stimulating experience. Research reveals that students who participate in interdisciplinary courses report not only greater gains in learning, but also higher levels of satisfaction with their learning experience (19, 270).

"Look at the *purposes* of the courses you choose, not just at their content."

—Robert Shoenberg, Senior Fellow, Association of American Colleges & Universities

"The frontiers of knowledge, both in scholarship and the world of work, now call for cross-disciplinary inquiry, analysis, and application. The major issues and problems of our time—from ensuring global sustainability to negotiating international markets to expanding human freedom—transcend individual disciplines."

—Association of American Colleges & Universities

Author's Experience—Joe Cuseo

When teaching my psychology courses, if I happened to mention something that related to something else that my students were discussing in another course, they would perk up and excitedly point out (or blurt out): "This is like what we were talking about in _____ (some other) class!" When my students got so excited about seeing a connection between courses, I was both impressed and depressed. On the one hand, I was happy they were making meaningful connections; on the other hand, seeing how surprised they were when they detected a connection made me realize that this was a rare experience. Consequently, I began making more intentional attempts to connect material in my psychology courses with ideas covered in other subject areas. I found that making these connections further increased student interest in the topics I was teaching. I became so interested in making connections between my field and other fields of study that I took a new teaching position at a college which emphasized interdisciplinary, team-taught courses. I went on to team-teach a variety of interdisciplinary courses such as: Humor and the Comic Spirit (combining psychology, literature, and film), Sports in American Society (psychology, sociology, and philosophy), Drug Use and Abuse (psychology and criminal justice), and Mind, Brain, and Behavior (psychology and biology). These courses provided me with some of my most powerful and memorable learning experiences.

If you have the opportunity to take an interdisciplinary course or participate in an interdisciplinary program, take advantage of it; you're likely to find it to be an enlightening and enjoyable experience.

Your campus may offer an interdisciplinary "senior seminar" or "capstone course" designed to integrate general education with your specialized major (85). If such a course is available on your campus, strongly consider taking it. It can help you "tie together" your college education and gain a synoptic perspective, enabling you to see how different disciplinary perspectives come together to form the "big picture."

If interdisciplinary courses are not offered on your campus, do your best to make connections between courses on your own. Always be on the lookout to combine the knowledge you acquire in different subject areas to get a more complete and coherent understanding of yourself and the world around you.

3. Use electives to complete a *minor* in a liberal arts field that complements your major.

Most campuses give students the option of completing a minor along with their major. A college minor usually requires about half the course credits required for a college major. Completing a minor in a field outside your major can strengthen your resume and promote your employment prospects; it demonstrates your versatility and enables you to acquire knowledge and skills that may be underemphasized in your major. For instance, students majoring in business or computer science may complete a minor in a Humanities subject to develop skills and perspectives that aren't strongly emphasized in their major (e.g., a minor in foreign language or international studies to enhance their career prospects in today's global economy).

If you decide to major in a liberal arts field, you can further increase your marketability by combining your major with a cluster of courses in a more "applied" pre-professional field. Employment and career opportunities for non-business majors may be enhanced by taking courses in business (271). For example, students majoring in the Fine Arts or Humanities may take courses in the fields of mathematics (e.g., statistics), technology (e.g., computer science), and business (e.g., marketing) to acquire knowledge and skills that are not typically emphasized by their major. Some campuses offer business courses that are designed specifically for liberal arts majors.

4. Use some of your electives to enroll in *service-learning* courses that connect learning in the classroom with service to the community.

When volunteer work is integrated into an academic course and students reflect on their volunteer experience through writing or speaking, it's referred to as *service learning*. Your campus likely offers courses that incorporate volunteer service in the local community and relates these service experiences to material covered in class (e.g., via writing assignments and class discussions). Research indicates that students who participate in service-learning courses make gains in multiple areas of self-development, including critical thinking and leadership (20, 267).

In addition to serving your community and promoting your personal development, service learning enables you to explore different work environments and gain work experience in career fields related to your area of service. For example, service performed for different age groups (children, adolescents, or the elderly) and in different work environments (hospital, school, or laboratory) provide you with résumé-building work experiences while simultaneously allowing you to test your interest in careers related to these age groups and work environments. Service experiences also enable you to network with professionals outside of college who can serve as personal references and supply you with letters of recommendation. Furthermore, if these off-campus contacts are impressed with your volunteer work, they may become interested in hiring you on a part-time basis while you're attending college or as a full-time employee after you graduate from college.

Author's Experience—Joe Cuseo

I was once advising two first-year students, Kim and Christopher. Kim was thinking about becoming a physical therapist and Chris was thinking about becoming an elementary school teacher. To test her interest in and aptitude for physical therapy, I suggested to Kim that she visit the hospital nearby our college to see whether she could do volunteer work in the physical therapy unit. The hospital did need volunteers, so she volunteered in the physical therapy unit and loved it. Her volunteer experience confirmed for her that physical therapy was the career she wanted to pursue. She went on to complete a degree in physical therapy and is now a professional physical therapist.

I suggested to Chris, the student who was thinking about becoming an elementary school teacher, that he visit some local schools to see whether they could use a teacher's aide. One of the schools needed his services, so Chris volunteered as a teacher's aide for about ten weeks. At about two weeks into his volunteer experience, he came to my office and told me that the kids were just about driving him crazy and that he was no longer interested in becoming a teacher! He ended up majoring in communications.

Kim and Chris were the first students I advised to get involved in volunteer work to test their career interests. Their volunteer experiences proved to be so valuable in helping them clarify their career goals that I continued to advise all my students to get volunteer experience in the field they were considering as a future career.

PAUSE FOR THOUGHT

Have you done volunteer work? If yes, did you learn anything about yourself or anything from your volunteer experiences that might help you identify careers that are compatible with your personal interests, talents, and values?
If no, what type of volunteer experience do you think would be most relevant to your career goals?

Be sure you understand the relationship between the major you're choosing and the careers associated with it. There are numerous misconceptions and myths about the relationship between majors and careers, some of which can lead students to make uninformed or unrealistic decisions about a college major. Following are four common myths about the major-career relationship that you should be aware of and factor into your decisions about a college major.

Myth 1: When you choose your major, you're choosing your career.

While some majors lead directly to a particular career, most do not. Majors leading directly to specialized careers are often called pre-professional or pre-vocational majors; they include such fields as accounting, engineering, and nursing. However, the relationship between most college majors and careers is often not direct or linear; you don't travel on a straight monorail from your major to one-and-only-one career that's directly connected to your major. For instance, all physics majors don't become physicists, all philosophy majors don't become philosophers, all history majors don't become historians, and all English majors don't become Englishmen (or Englishwomen). Instead, the same major typically leads you to a variety of career options.

The truth is that the trip from a college major to eventual career(s) is less like scaling a pole and more like climbing a tree. As illustrated in **Figure 5.1**, you begin with the tree's trunk (the foundation provided by the liberal arts), which leads to separate limbs (choices for college majors), which, in turn, leads to different branches (different career paths or options). Note that the different sets of branches (careers) grow from the same limb (major).

Similarly, different career clusters or "career families" grow from the same major. For example, a major in English can lead to a variety of careers that involve writing (e.g., editing, journalism, or publishing) and a major in art can lead to different careers that involve visual media (e.g., illustration, graphic design, or art therapy). Furthermore, different majors can lead to the same career. For instance, many different majors can lead a student to law school and a career as a lawyer; in fact, there's really no such thing as a "law major" or "pre-law major." Also, students can enter medical school with a variety of majors (or minors) as long as they have a solid set of foundational courses in biology and chemistry and do well on the medical-college admissions test.

The mistaken belief that your major becomes your career probably accounts for the fact that 58 percent of college graduates major in a pre-professional or pre-vocational field such as nursing, accounting, or engineering (18). Each of these majors leads to a specific career

> "Linear thinking can keep you from thinking broadly about your options and being open-minded to new opportunities."
>
> —Karen Brooks, author, *You Majored in What?*

> "I intend on becoming a corporate lawyer. I am an English major. The reason I chose this major is because while I was researching the educational backgrounds of some corporate attorneys, I found that a lot were English majors. It helps with writing and delivering cases."
>
> —College sophomore

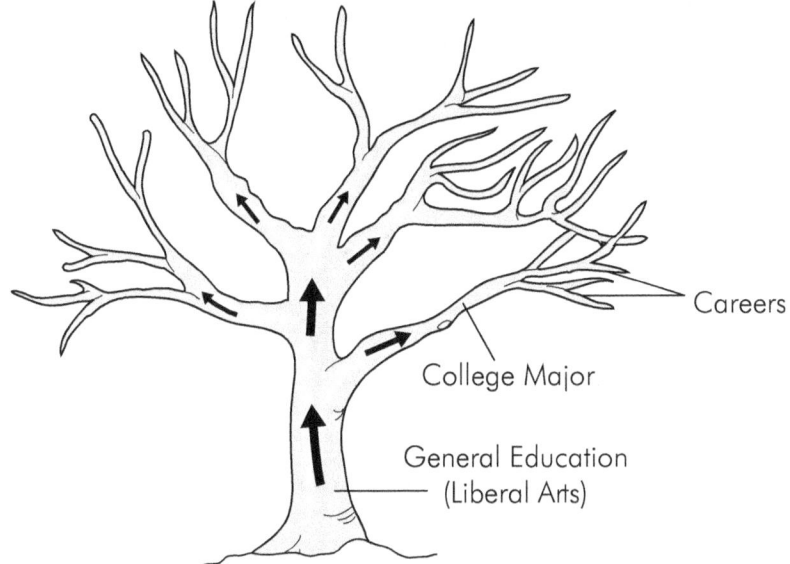

FIGURE 5.1

The Relationship between General Education (Liberal Arts), College Majors, and Careers

that's directly connected to it, which reassures students (and their parents) that they will have a job after graduation. Although it's true that students in pre-professional majors are more likely to be hired *immediately* after graduation, college graduates with other college majors are just as likely to be hired within six months after graduation and they're not more vulnerable to unemployment. (129, 130, 232). Additional research indicates that college graduates change jobs multiple times during their first two decades of work following graduation, and the further they proceed along their career path, the more likely they are to be working in a field that's unrelated to their college major (192).

Although it's important to think about your choice of a college major and your career choice at the same time, for most college students these are different choices made at different times. Choosing your major represents a more immediate decision; choosing your career path is a decision that comes later. When you choose a college major, you're not making a commitment to a career that you'll be doing for the remainder of your working life.

Myth 2: If you want to continue your education after a bachelor's degree, you must continue in the same field as your college major.

After college graduation, two primary paths are immediately available to you: (1) enter the workforce directly, or (2) continue your education in graduate school or professional school. (See **Figure 5.2** for a visual map of the stages and milestones in the college experience and the paths available to you after college.)

> "The first week of law school, one of my professors stressed the importance of 'researching, analyzing and writing.' I thought this was an interesting thing to say, because English majors learn and practice these skills in every class."
>
> —English major attending law school (288)

Once you attain a bachelor's degree, you can continue your education in a field that's not directly related to your college major. This is particularly true for students majoring in liberal arts fields that don't funnel them directly into one specific career after graduation (232). For example, if you major in English, you can still go to graduate school in a subject other than English, or go to law school, or get a master's degree in business administration. In fact, most students attending graduate school in the field of business (e.g., MBA programs) were not business majors in college (96).

Myth 3: You should major in business because most college graduates work in business organizations.

The majority of college graduates who work in business settings did not graduate with a business major. It is this mistaken belief that likely accounts for the fact that business continues to be the most popular major among college students (210, 299). Students (and their parents) see most college graduates employed in business settings and conclude that if students are going to work for a business, they better major in business. If you have an interest in and passion for pursuing business as a major, by all means major in business. However, don't choose to major in business by thinking it's the only major that will qualify you to work for a business after you graduate from college.

Myth 4: If you major in a liberal arts field, the only career available to you is teaching.

A commonly held myth is that all you can do with a major in a liberal arts field is to teach the subject you majored in (e.g., English majors

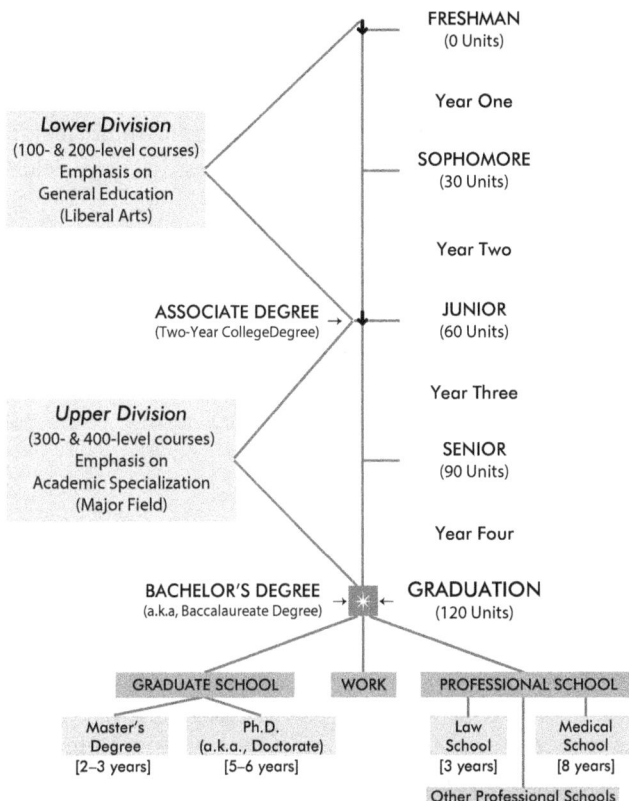

FIGURE 5.2

A Snapshot of the College Experience and Beyond

Notes

1. On average, about one-third of the courses required for a college degree are general education courses selected from the liberal arts curriculum (76). However, the number of required general education courses varies from campus to campus and can vary at the same campus depending on the student's major.
2. The word "freshman" originated in England in 1596, when every college student was a "fresh" (new) "man." Today, the term "freshman" is frequently being replaced by "first-year student" because this a more gender-neutral term.
3. The term "baccalaureate" derives from "Bacchus"—the Greed god of wine and festive celebration, and "laurel"—a wreath made from the laurel plant that ancient Greeks draped around the neck of Olympic champions.
4. It often takes college students longer than four years to graduate due to a variety of reasons, such as working part-time and taking fewer courses per term, needing to repeat courses that were failed or dropped, or making a late change to a different major and needing to fulfill additional requirements for the new major.
5. Graduate and professional schools are options for continuing to higher levels of education after completion of an undergraduate (college) education.
6. Students going to graduate school on a full-time bassis can sometimes support themselves financially by working part-time as a teaching assistant (TA) or research assistant (RA). It is also possible to enroll in some graduate or professional school programs on a part-time basis, while holding a full-time job.
7. The term "Ph.D." refers to "Doctor of Philosophy," respecting the fact that the first scholars were the ancient Greek philosophers (e.g., Socrates, Plato, and Aristotle). However, a Ph.D. can be earned in many different academic fields (Mathematics, Music, Economic, etc.)
8. Compared to graduate school, professional school involves advanced education in more "applied" professions (e.g., pharmacy or public administration).

CHAPTER 5: Tying It All Together

become English teachers; history majors become history teachers). The truth is that students majoring in different fields in the liberal arts proceed to enter, advance, and prosper in a wide variety of careers. Among students graduating from college with liberal arts majors who went on to achieve professional success in career fields other than teaching include:

- Jill Barad (English major), former CEO, Mattel Toys
- Steve Case (political science major), former CEO, America Online
- Brian Lamb (speech major), former CEO, C-Span
- Willie Brown (liberal studies major), former Mayor of San Francisco (146)

Significant numbers of liberal arts majors are also employed in positions relating to marketing, human resources, and public affairs (40, 286). An experienced career counselor once tracked the majors of college graduates working in the insurance industry. She found an art history major working at a major insurance firm whose job was to value oriental carpets and art holdings. She also found a geology major working for an insurance company whose job was to evaluate beach properties and determine the odds of hurricanes or other natural phenomena causing property damage. This former geology major spent much of her work time traveling to beachfront communities to review new developments and assessing damages after hurricanes or other tragic events (51). Research also reveals that the career mobility and career advancement of liberal arts majors working in the corporate world are comparable to business majors. For example, liberal arts majors are just as likely to advance to the highest levels of corporate leadership as majors in such pre-professional fields as business and engineering (232).

KEY POINT

The liberal arts broaden, rather than narrow, your future vocational choices; they open up doors to a variety of careers. If you have a passion for and talent in a liberal arts field, consider majoring in it. Don't be dismayed or discouraged by those who may question your choice by asking: "What are you going to do with a degree in that major?"

Also, don't be discouraged if you discover college graduates with liberal arts majors earning lower starting salaries than majors in pre-professional fields. Research indicates that over the course of their working lives, liberal arts majors earn as much as graduates with pre-professional majors. The transferable, lifelong-learning skills developed by the liberal arts become lifelong *earning* skills whose economic benefits increase in later stages of a person's career (132, 232). Another reason why the lifetime earnings of liberal arts majors are comparable to majors in pre-professional fields is that liberal arts majors are more likely to go on to graduate school; about 40 percent of them eventually earn a master's or doctoral degree (269).

Author's Experience—Joe Cuseo

My brother Vinny was a philosophy major in college. He came home one Christmas wearing a t-shirt on which was printed the message: "Philosophy major. Will think for food." With his major in philosophy, my brother went to graduate school, completed a master's degree in higher education, and is now making a six-figure salary working as a college administrator. Looking back, his old t-shirt should have read: "Philosophy major. Will think for money."

> **KEY POINT**
>
> A higher starting salary immediately after graduation doesn't necessarily translate into higher lifetime income. In the world of work, it's not how fast you start, but how steady you advance and how strong you finish.

Engage in co-curricular experiences on campus to complement your course work. Participating in student clubs, campus organizations, and other types of co-curricular activities can provide you with a valuable source of experiential learning to augment classroom-based learning. Keep in mind that *academic* experiences and *educational* experiences are not synonymous. The former refers to course-related

> "The key to making your college learning experience as valuable as possible is 'coherence'—the integration of the academic and extracurricular components of your undergraduate education."
>
> —Robert Shoenberg, Senior Fellow, Association of American Colleges & Universities

learning acquired through reading and listening to professors share their knowledge. Educational experiences are broader; they include academic (classroom-based) learning and *experiential* learning—that is, learning from direct, "hands-on" experience which can take place in a variety of out-of-class (co-curricular) settings. A sizable body of research points to the power of co-curricular experiences for promoting learning, personal development, and career success (19, 172, 231, 232, 134). Thus, a well-rounded education includes both academic and experiential learning. Make every effort you can to complement your classroom-based learning with out-of-class learning experiences, particularly those that:

- allow you to develop leadership skills (e.g., leadership retreats, student government, college committees, peer mentoring, and peer tutoring);
- enable you to interact with students from diverse ethnic and racial groups (e.g., multicultural or international clubs and student organizations); and
- provide you with out-of-class experiences related to the college major or career you've chosen or are exploring (e.g., participating in student clubs in your major, or engaging in undergraduate research with a faculty member in your major field of study).

Keep in mind that co-curricular experiences are also career-building experiences, so be sure to keep track of these experiences and showcase them in your resume, letters of application, and personal interviews. Lastly, don't forget that the campus professionals with whom you interact while participating in co-curricular activities (e.g., Director of Student Life or Dean of Students) may serve as personal references and sources of letters of recommendation to future employers and graduate or professional schools.

Gain *internship* experience. Internships represent a form of experiential learning for which you may receive academic credit or financial compensation. A major advantage of internships is that they enable you to avoid the typical "catch-22" scenario encountered by college graduates when they interview for their first career position after graduation. A potential employer asks: "What work experience have you had in this field?" The graduate responds: "I haven't had any work experience because I've been a full-time student." You can sidestep this deflating scenario by completing an internship while in college; it will enable you to beat the "no experience" rap after graduation and help differentiate you from other job applicants.

National surveys reveal that employers seek college graduates who are not just knowledgeable, but who can *apply* the knowledge they've acquired (136). More than 75 percent of employers prefer college graduates with internships (208) and those graduates who've had internship experiences while in college are more likely to find immediate employment after college graduation (232, 134). It's especially important for liberal arts majors to actively seek out and gain internship experience because unlike pre-professional majors (e.g., nursing and engineering), liberal arts majors don't have internships or field work already built into their program of study.

Internships are typically available to college students during their junior or senior year; however, some campuses offer internships for first- and second-year students. Check with your Career Center if this opportunity is available to you. You can also pursue internships on your own, by searching for internships on the Web, or by consulting published guides that list internship opportunities and provide information on how to apply for them (e.g., *Peterson's Internships* and the *Vault Guide to Top Internships*). Information on internships may also be available from the Chamber of Commerce in your hometown or in the local community where your college is located.

"The world's economy no longer pays for what people know but for what they can do with what they know."

—Andreas Schleicher, Deputy Director of Education, Organization for Economic Cooperation and Development

"Give me a history major who has done internships and a business major who hasn't, and I'll hire the history major every time."

—William Adrery, senior vice president, Investor Communications Company

Developing an Action Plan for Infusing Diversity into Your College Experience

You can increase the impact of the liberal arts on your personal and professional development by intentionally infusing diversity into your educational plan. Here is a systematic set of strategies for doing so.

Incorporate diversity courses into your planned schedule of courses. Review your college catalog (bulletin) and identify courses that are designed to promote understanding or appreciation of diversity. These courses may focus on diverse cultures found within the United States—sometimes referred to as multicultural courses, or diverse cultures associated with different countries—sometimes referred to as international or cross-cultural courses.

In a national study of college students who experienced multicultural courses, it was discovered that students of all racial and ethnic groups made significant gains in learning and intellectual development (264, 265). These findings are reinforced by results from a survey of undergraduate students at Pennsylvania State University, which revealed that students who participated in multicultural courses experienced gains in both knowledge and appreciation of diversity; for example, both white students and students of color developed more tolerant attitudes about racial and gender differences (229).

Taking courses focusing on international diversity can help you develop the global perspective needed for success in today's international economy and strengthen your college transcript (51, 88, 207). (To help you develop a systematic plan for infusing multicultural and international courses into your college coursework see Chapter 5 Exercise.) The need for college graduates to acquire an international perspective, cross-cultural awareness, and intercultural competence is probably more important today than at any other time in history. Yet American college students lag behind students from other industrialized nations in international knowledge and second-language skills (40).

PAUSE FOR THOUGHT

What other language(s) do you wish you were able to speak? Why?

Be on the lookout for diversity implications associated with topics you're reading about or discussing in class. Consider the multicultural and cross-cultural ramifications of material you're studying and use examples of diversity to support or illustrate your points. If you're allowed to choose a topic for a research project, select one that relates to diversity or has implications for diversity.

Take foreign language courses. Only 5 to10 percent of American college graduates have basic competence in any language other than English, and approximately two-thirds of them have not taken a single course in international studies (4). Taking courses that develop your ability to comprehend and communicate in a different language not only benefit you educationally, but also professionally. Research repeatedly shows that employers value college graduates with foreign language skills (52, 137, 108, 225). Furthermore, "second language study opens the door for native speakers to view their own language in perspective, to understand their own culture from another point of view. This enhanced perspective allows a greater appreciation not only of English vocabulary and language usage but of the American cultural tradition and its values" (76).

Author's Experience—Joe Cuseo

A few years ago, I had the opportunity to make a presentation at an international conference in Belgium. There were participants there from different European countries, all of whom spoke and understood English, and most of whom spoke at least two languages. Many of the Belgians I met actually were fluent in more than three languages.

While I enjoyed the conference and learned much from the international scholars who I met, I was also very humbled and embarrassed to be among the very few people present who was monolingual. It made me think that if I could do college all over again, I would have used some of my elective courses to learn a second language.

Strategies for Increasing Personal Contact and Interpersonal Interaction with Members of Diverse Groups

> "Actual interaction with peers of different races is far superior to merely reading or watching a movie about racial issues."
>
> —Spokesperson for General Motors Corporation commenting on the company's experience with employees (68)

Studies show that appreciating diversity is maximized when students not only acquire knowledge about diversity, which represents *vicarious* learning that's obtained from someone else—such as hearing a lecturer and reading and author—but also by learning that takes places—in other words, *experiential* learning (203). Formal courses and academic programs can help you learn *about* diversity; firsthand interaction with diverse people enables you to learn *from* diversity. There's a big difference between acquiring knowledge of another country by reading about it, as opposed to going to the country and actually interacting with its natives. Interpersonal interaction with individuals from diverse groups moves you beyond acquiring cultural knowledge to developing intercultural competence.

Research shows that people are much more likely to develop relationships with others whose prior experiences and cultural backgrounds are similar to their own (287). This tendency is growing because more Americans are choosing to live in neighborhoods with others who share their own cultural, political, and religious viewpoints (36).

> "I am very happy with the diversity here, but it also frightens me. I have never been in a situation where I have met people who are Jewish, Muslim, atheist, born-again, and many more."
>
> —First-year student (101)

The diversity that exists on your campus represents a golden opportunity for you to break the habit of associating only with people similar to you. Seize this opportunity to diversify your social network by making an intentional effort to interact with and learn from people who are different than you.

Your initial comfort level when interacting with people from diverse groups is likely to depend on how much prior experience you've had with diversity. If you've had little or no previous contact with members of diverse groups, it may be more challenging for you to initiate interactions with diverse students on campus. However, the good news is that students with the least prior experience with diversity are those who gain the most from experiencing it. Research consistently

Humanity, Diversity, and the Liberal Arts: Foundation of a College Education

demonstrates that when humans encounter people and experiences that differ radically from their prior experiences, they make the greatest gains in learning and cognitive development (3, 241).

Following are specific strategies for increasing interpersonal contact and collaboration with individuals from diverse groups.

Take advantage of social media to "chat" virtually with students from diverse groups on your own campus, or students on other campuses. Electronic communication can be a convenient and comfortable way to initially interact with members of diverse groups with whom you have had little prior experience. After you've communicated *online*, you're more likely to feel more comfortable about interacting *in person*.

Engage in co-curricular experiences involving diversity. Review your student handbook to find co-curricular programs, student activities, student clubs, or campus organizations that emphasize diversity awareness and appreciation. Studies indicate that participation in co-curricular experiences relating to diversity promotes critical thinking (232) and reduces unconscious prejudice (37).

If your campus sponsors multicultural or cross-cultural retreats, strongly consider participating in them. A retreat setting can provide a comfortable environment in which you can get to interact personally with diverse students without being distracted by your customary social circle and daily routine.

> "Empirical evidence shows that the actual effects on student development of emphasizing diversity and of student participation in diversity activities are overwhelmingly positive."
>
> —Alexander Astin, *What Matters in College*

Place yourself in situations and locations on campus where you will come in regular contact with individuals from diverse groups. Research in social psychology shows that relationships are more likely to form among people who come in regular contact with one another (175), and research on diversity shows that when there's regular contact between members of different racial or ethnic groups, stereotyping is sharply reduced and intercultural friendships are more likely to develop (238, 239). You can create these conditions by making an intentional attempt to sit near diverse students in the classroom, library, or student café, and by joining them for class discussion groups or group projects. Also, consider spending time at the multicultural center on your campus, or becoming a member of a campus club or organization that's devoted to diversity awareness (e.g., multicultural or international student club). This will enable you to make regular contact with members of cultural groups other than your own; it also sends a clear message to them that you value diversity because you've taken the initiative to connect with them on "their turf."

If you are given the opportunity to form your own discussion groups and group-project teams, join or create groups composed of students from diverse backgrounds. You can gain greater exposure to diverse perspectives by intentionally joining or forming learning groups of students who differ in terms of gender, age, race, or ethnicity. Including diversity in your discussion groups not only provides social variety, it also enriches the quality of group work by allowing members to gain access to and learn from multiple perspectives. For instance, in learning groups that are diverse with respect to age, older students will bring a broad range of life experiences that younger students can draw upon and learn from, while younger students can provide a more contemporary and idealistic perspective to the group's discussions. Gender diversity is also likely to infuse group discussions with different learning styles and ways of understanding issues. Studies show that males are more likely to be "separate knowers" who tend to "detach" themselves from the concept or issue being discussed so they can analyze it. In contrast, females are more likely to be "connected knowers" who tend to relate personally to concepts and connect them with their own experiences and the experiences of others. For example, when interpreting a poem, males are more likely to ask: "What techniques can I use to analyze it?" In contrast, females would be more likely to ask: "What is the poet trying to say to me?" (28). It's also been found that females are more likely to work collaboratively during group discussions and collect the ideas of other members; in contrast, males are more likely to adopt a competitive approach and debate the ideas of others (187). Both of these styles of learning are valuable and you can capitalize on them by forming gender-diverse discussion groups.

Forming discussion groups with members of different races and cultures can reduce prejudice and promote intercultural appreciation, but only if each member's cultural identity and perspective is sought and valued by the discussion group (26). Seeking out divergent (diverse) viewpoints has been found to be one of the best ways to develop critical thinking skills (147, 173). During group discussions, you can demonstrate leadership by seeking out views and opinions of classmates from diverse backgrounds and ensuring that the ideas of people from minority groups are included and respected. Also, after class discussions, you can ask students from different backgrounds if there was any point made or position taken in class that they would have strongly questioned or challenged.

If there is little or no diversity among students in class, encourage your classmates to look at the topic or issue they're discussing from diverse perspectives. For instance, you might ask: "If there were international students here, what might they be adding to our discussion?" or, "If members of certain minority groups were here, would they be offering a different viewpoint?"

"The classroom can provide a 'public place' where community can be practiced."

—Susanne Morse,
Renewing Civic Capacity: Preparing College Students for Service and Citizenship

PAUSE FOR THOUGHT

What do you think distinguishes group work from teamwork?

Form collaborative learning teams with students from diverse backgrounds. A learning *team* is more than a discussion group; it moves beyond discussion to *collaboration*—its members "co-labor" (work together) to reach the same learning goal. Research from kindergarten through college indicates that when students collaborate in teams, their academic performance and interpersonal skills are strengthened (84). Also, when individuals from different racial groups work collaboratively toward the same goal, racial prejudice is reduced and interracial friendships are more likely to be formed (5,

11, 56, 94). These positive developments may be explained, in part, by the fact that when members of diverse ethnic and racial groups come together on the same team, nobody is a member of an "out" group ("them"); instead, everybody belongs to the same "in" group ("us") (244, 262).

Characteristics of effective learning teams are summarized in **Box 5.1**. In an analysis of multiple studies involving more than 90,000 people from twenty-five different countries, it was found that when interaction between members of diverse groups takes place under the conditions listed here, prejudice is significantly reduced (240); moreover, these are the very same conditions that promote the greatest gains in learning (152, 263).

> **BOX 5.1**
>
> **Tips for Teamwork:**
> **Creating Diverse and Effective Learning Teams**
>
> 1. **Intentionally include students with different cultural backgrounds and life experiences when forming learning teams and study groups.** Teaming-up only with friends or classmates whose backgrounds and experiences are similar to you can actually impair your team's performance because teammates can get off track and onto topics that have nothing to do with the learning task (e.g., what they did last weekend or what they're planning to do next weekend).
> 2. **Before jumping into group work, take some time to interact informally with your teammates.** If team members have the opportunity for some social "warm up" time (e.g., to learn each other's names and learn something about each other), they'll feel more comfortable about expressing their ideas and develop a stronger sense of team identity, particularly if they come from diverse (and unfamiliar) cultural backgrounds. This feeling of group solidarity can create a foundation of trust among group members, enabling them to work together as a team.

A sense of team trust may be increased further by having teamwork take place in a friendly, informal setting. The context in which a group interacts can influence the nature and quality of their interaction. Group members are more likely to interact openly and collaboratively when they work in an environment that's conducive to relationship building. A living room or a lounge area provides a warmer and friendlier team-learning atmosphere than a sterile classroom.

3. **Have your team create a single work product that they develop together.** This product should reflect the team's collective effort and joint achievement (e.g., a completed sheet of answers to questions, or a comprehensive list of ideas). Creating a common final product helps keep individuals thinking in terms of "we" (not "me") and keeps the team moving in the same direction toward the same goal.

4. **Group members should work interdependently—depending on each other to reach their common goal and have equal opportunity to contribute to the team's final product.** Each team member should take responsibility for making an indispensable contribution to the team's end product, such as contributing (1) a different piece of *information* (e.g., a specific chapter from the textbook or a particular section of class notes), (2) a particular form of *thinking* to the learning task (e.g., analysis, synthesis, or application), or (3) a different *perspective* (e.g., national, international, or global). Said in another way, each group member should be responsible for bringing a different piece that's needed to complete the whole puzzle. Similar to a sports team, all members of a learning team should also have specific roles or functions to play during the process of group work. For instance, each teammate could assume one of the following roles:

> TEAM = Together Everyone Achieves More
>
> —Author Unknown

* **Manager**—whose role is to ensure that the team stays on track and moving toward its goal
* **Moderator**—whose role is to ensure that all teammates have equal opportunity to contribute
* **Summarizer**—whose role is to monitor the team's progress, to identify what's been accomplished and what still needs to be done
* **Recorder**—whose role is to keep a written record of the team's ideas

When contact among people from diverse groups takes place under the four conditions described in this box, group work is transformed into teamwork and acquires the potential to promote higher learning and deeper appreciation of diversity. A win-win scenario is created: learning and thinking are strengthened while bias and prejudice are weakened (6, 10, 15, 54, 77, 259).

KEY POINT Capitalize on the power of team learning by teaming up with peers from diverse backgrounds. Simply stated, we learn more from people who differ from us than we do from people similar to us.

After concluding work in diverse learning teams, take time to reflect on the experience. The final step in any learning process, whether it be learning from a lecture or learning from a group discussion, is to step back from the process and thoughtfully review it. Deep learning requires not only effortful action but also thoughtful reflection (38, 250). You can reflect on your experiences with diverse learning groups by asking yourself questions that prompt you to think about the ideas shared by members of your group and the impact those ideas had on you. For instance, you could ask yourself (and your teammates) the following questions:

- What major similarities in viewpoints did all group members share? (What were the common themes?)
- What major differences of opinion were expressed by diverse members of our group? (What were the variations on the themes?)
- Were there particular topics or issues raised during the discussion that provoked intense reactions or emotional responses from certain members of our group?
- Did the group discussion lead any individuals to change their mind about an idea or position they originally held?

Engage in volunteer experiences that allow you to work in diverse communities or neighborhoods. Volunteering in communities beyond the borders of your campus may give you the opportunity to interact with diverse groups of people who are not well represented within your campus community. Your volunteer opportunities in diverse settings can strengthen your resume and enable you to network with professionals in the work world who can serve as personal resources, references, and sources for letters of recommendation. In addition, volunteer experiences can function as "exploratory internships," giving you the opportunity to gain diversity experience while simultaneously allowing you to gain experience and information on career fields you may pursue after college. Most importantly, volunteering instills feelings of pride and self-fulfillment about making a difference in someone else's life. Studies show that people who devote time to doing good things for others report higher levels of personal "happiness" and life satisfaction (199).

PAUSE FOR THOUGHT

If you were to do engage in volunteer work or community service in the future that would allow you to work with diverse groups of people, where would you choose to do it? Why?

Attempt to find an *internship* in a company or organization that allows you the opportunity to work with people from diverse backgrounds and cultures. Hands-on experience with diversity not only promotes learning, it also enhances your job prospects by enabling you to develop intercultural skills needed for success in today's multicultural work world. Because America's workforce is more diverse now than at any other time in our nation's history, you'll likely find yourself working with employers, employees, co-workers, customers, and clients from diverse cultural backgrounds in whatever career you pursue.

If possible, participate in a study-abroad or travel-study program that gives you the opportunity to live in another country and interact directly with its native citizens. In addition to coursework, you can gain international knowledge and a global perspective by participating in a program that enables you to actually *experience* a different country. You can do this for a full term or for a shorter time period (e.g., January, May, or summer term). To prepare for international experiences, take a course in the language, culture, or history of the nation to which you will be traveling.

Research on students who participate in study-abroad programs indicates that these experiences promote greater appreciation of cross-cultural differences, greater interest in world affairs, and greater commitment to peace and international cooperation (40, 158). Additional research shows that study abroad has benefits for students' personal development, including improved self-confidence, sense of independence, and ability to function in complex environments (64, 145).

Keep a *journal* to record personal reflections on what you've learned from your experiences with diversity. Learning from any experience is strengthened when you write about it because writing increases your level of involvement with the experience and your ability to reflect deeply on it. The phrase "writing to learn" has been coined by scholars to capture the idea that writing is not only a communication skill learned in English composition classes; it's also a learning skill that deepens your understanding of any academic subject or life experience that you write about, including your experiences with diversity. Thus, writing can be used not only as a vehicle for communicating

> "I remember that my self-image was being influenced by the media. I got the impression that women had to look a certain way. I dyed my hair, wore different clothes, more makeup . . . all because magazines, TV, [and] music videos 'said' that was beautiful. Luckily, when I went to Brazil and saw a different, more natural beauty, I came back to America more as myself. I let go of the hold the [American] media image had on me."
>
> —First-year college student

your knowledge or ideas to others; it can also be used as a tool for strengthening your own learning and thinking (2, 14, 99, 300).

When recording diversity reflections in your journal, keep the following questions in mind:

- What type of feelings or emotions did I experience?
- When and where did I experience these feelings? (What was the situation or context?)
- Why did I experience these feelings?
- Did the experience alter my beliefs, attitudes, or opinions in any way?
- Is the experience likely to have any impact on my future behavior or actions?

> "I write to understand as much as to be understood."
>
> —Elie Wiesel, world-renown novelist, Nobel Prize winner, and Holocaust survivor

Tying It Altogether: Reflecting on Your College Experiences

Students often think it's the final product (a college diploma) that provides them with a passport to a good job and career success (18, 268). However, more important than the end product is the process—the learning experience that led to the product. When you're engaged in the process of college learning, it may appear that you're just developing academic skills, but you're actually developing skills for lifelong learning and career success. Don't forget that the learning skills you acquire in college are transferable to multiple life roles beyond college.

For most employers of college graduates, what matters more than the credential earned or the list of courses you completed are the skills and personal qualities the job applicant brings to the position (98, 107). You can start building these skills and qualities through effective *self-monitoring*—that is, monitoring (watching) yourself and keeping track of the skills you're using and developing during your college experience. Skills are mental habits, and like other habits that are repeatedly practiced, their development can be so gradual and subtle that you may not even notice how much growth has taken place (like watching grass grow). Thus, career development specialists recommend that you consciously reflect on the skills you're using so that you remain aware of their development and be ready to articulate or "sell" them to potential employers (181).

One strategy that can be used to track your developing skills is to keep a *learning journal* in which you reflect on the academic tasks and assignments you've completed, along with the skills you developed while completing them. Also, include skills that you've developed outside the classroom, such as those used during co-curricular experiences, volunteer services, part-time jobs, and personal hobbies.

Since skills are actions, it's best to record them as verbs in your journal. You're likely to find that many of these actions will be the same ones that employers will seek in the workforce. **Box 5.2** contains a sample of action-oriented career skills you're likely to develop in college that are relevant to successful performance in a variety of careers.

BOX 5.2

Personal Skills Relevant to Successful Career Performance

The following behaviors represent a sample of useful skills that are relevant to success in various careers (107, 41). As you track your learning experiences in college, remain mindful of whether you're developing these or other skills, both inside and outside the classroom.

advise	evaluate	research
assemble	explain	resolve
calculate	initiate	sort
coach	measure	summarize
coordinate	motivate	supervise
create	negotiate	synthesize
delegate	present	
design	produce	

In addition to tracking skills, keep track of positive traits and attributes you're developing. While skills are best recorded as action verbs because they represent actions that you can perform for anyone who hires you, personal attributes are best recorded as *adjectives* because they describe who you are and what positive qualities you can bring to any position. **Box 5.3** identifies examples of personal traits and attributes that are relevant to successful performance in any career.

KEY POINT

Keeping track of your developing skills and attributes is as important to your future success as completing courses and compiling credits. Get in the habit of stepping back from your learning experiences, reflecting on the skills and qualities you're developing, and making note of them before they slip your mind.

BOX 5.3

Personal Traits and Attributes Relevant to Successful Career Performance in Any Career

As you proceed through college, keep track of these and other personal attributes or character traits you develop during the course of your college experience.

collaborative	imaginative	prepared
conscientious	industrious	productive
considerate	loyal	prudent
curious	observant	punctual
dependable	open-minded	reflective
determined	outgoing	sincere
energetic	patient	tactful
enthusiastic	persuasive	team player
ethical	positive	thorough
flexible	precise	thoughtful

CHAPTER 5: Tying It All Together

Begin building a personal *portfolio* that illustrates and documents your development. You may have heard the word "portfolio" in reference to a collection of artwork that professional artists put together to showcase or advertise their work. However, a portfolio has a broader meaning; it can be a collection of any material that depicts your skills and talents, or that demonstrates your educational and personal development. For example, a portfolio could include these items:

- Outstanding papers, exam performances, research projects, and lab reports
- Artwork and photos from study-abroad experiences, service learning, and internships
- Video footage of oral presentations and public performances
- Performance evaluations you've received from professors, student development professionals, and employers
- Letters of recognition or commendation from professors, student development professionals, and employers.

The ritual of burning completed coursework in high school is not recommended in college. Instead, save your best work, and include it in a personal portfolio.

You can start building a portfolio by using the broadening perspectives developed by the liberal arts as category headings under which you can organize your learning experiences and acquired skills. (See Chapter 1 Exercise in the Appendix.) These perspectives can serve as a skeletal outline for your portfolio that you can "flesh out" later with specific skills and attributes you've acquired over the course of your college experience.

Start saving your best work products and your reflections on those products. Store them in a traditional portfolio folder, save them on a computer disc to create an electronic portfolio, or create a website and upload your materials there. National surveys show that more than four of five employers believe that an electronic portfolio is useful in helping them ensure that the job applicants they hire have the knowledge and skills needed to succeed in their company or organization (136).

If you develop a skeletal plan now and faithfully flesh it out as you proceed through your college experience, at college graduation you will have a solid final product that demonstrates you're a college graduate with transferable skills who is well-rounded, globally minded, and interculturally competent.

Internet Resources

For additional information related to the ideas discussed in this chapter, see the following websites:

"What can I do with my liberal arts degree?" :
    http://www.bls.gov/ooq/2007/winter/art.01pdf
Internships:
    www.internships.com
    www.vaultreports.com
Diversity-related internship opportunities:
    National Diversity Internship Program (NDIP):
    mycareertva.va.gov
Benefits and challenges of experiencing diversity in college:
    wiseli.engr.wisc

Chapter Summary and Highlights

With some careful forethought, you can develop a plan for general education that maximizes the power of the liberal arts and the return on your investment in a college education. This chapter catalogues multiple strategies for developing such a plan, which are summarized below:

Enroll in courses that expose you to each of the broadening social–spatial and chronological perspectives developed by the liberal arts. These perspectives may be used as checklists to ensure that you are taking a comprehensive, multiple perspective view of any topic or issue you're studying.

If you're uncertain about a college major or minor, use your general education requirements to test your interests and talents in fields that you might choose as a major or minor. This strategy will allow you to explore your interest and ability in the subject while simultaneously fulfilling general education requirements for graduation.

Choose elective courses to:
- develop *transferable, durable* skills that can be used across the curriculum and throughout life;
- gain an *interdisciplinary* perspective on topics and issues;
- complete a *minor* in a liberal arts field that can complement your major; and
- enroll in *service-learning* courses that connect learning in the classroom with service to the community.

Be sure you understand the relationship between the major you're choosing and the careers associated with it. There are four common myths about the major-career relationship that you should be aware of and factor into your decisions about a college major:

Myth: When you choose your major, you're choosing your career.

Reality: While some majors lead directly to a particular career, most do not. The relationship between most college majors and careers is often not direct or linear; different career clusters or "career families" grow from the same major. Furthermore, different majors can lead to the same career.

Myth: If you want to continue your education after a bachelor's degree, you must continue in the same field as your college major.

Reality: Once you attain a bachelor's degree, you can continue your education in a field that's not directly related to your college major. This is particularly true for students majoring in liberal arts fields that don't funnel them directly into one specific career after graduation.

Myth: You should major in business because most college graduates work in business organizations.

Reality: The majority of college graduates working in business settings did not graduate with a business major.

Myth: If you major in a liberal arts field, the only career available to you is teaching.

Reality: Students majoring in different fields in the liberal arts proceed to enter, advance, and prosper in a wide variety of careers, including positions relating to marketing, human resources, and public affairs.

Engage in co-curricular experiences on campus to complement your course work. A well-rounded education includes both academic and experiential learning. Co-curricular experiences are also career-building experiences; keep track of these experiences and showcase them in your resume, letters of application, and personal interviews.

Gain internship experience. The overwhelming majority of employers prefer college graduates with internships and those graduates who've had internship experiences while in college are more likely to find immediate employment after college graduation. It's especially important for liberal arts majors to actively seek out and gain internship experience because unlike pre-professional majors (e.g., nursing and engineering), liberal arts majors don't have internships or field work already built into their program of study.

Develop an action plan for infusing diversity into your college experience. The impact of the liberal arts on your personal and professional development will be strengthened by using the following strategies to infuse diversity into your education plan.

- Incorporate diversity courses into your planned schedule of courses.
- Be on the lookout for diversity implications associated with topics you're reading about or discussing in class.
- Engage in co-curricular experiences involving diversity.
- Take advantage of social media to "chat" virtually with students from diverse groups on your own campus, or students on other campuses.
- Place yourself in situations and locations on campus where you will come in regular contact with individuals from diverse groups.
- Form discussion groups, group-project teams, and study groups with students from diverse backgrounds.
- Engage in volunteer experiences that allow you to work in diverse communities or neighborhoods.
- Attempt to find an internship in a company or organization that allows you the opportunity to work with people from diverse backgrounds and cultures.
- If possible, participate in a study-abroad or travel-study program that gives you the opportunity to live in another country and interact directly with its native citizens.
- Keep a journal to record personal reflections on what you've learned from your experiences with diversity.

Keep track of the skills and personal attributes you're developing in college and record them in a portfolio. This is as important to your future success as completing courses and compiling credits. Start saving your best work products and your reflections on those products. Store them in a traditional portfolio folder, save them on a computer disc to create an electronic portfolio, or create a website and upload your materials there. By the time you graduate, you should have a solid final product that demonstrates you're a college graduate with transferable skills who is well rounded, globally minded, and interculturally competent.

Questions and Final Reflections

1. Based on his research, psychologist Howard Gardner has identified the following multiple forms of intelligence.
   (a) Which of these types of intelligence do you think represents your strongest talent(s)?
   (b) Which college major(s) do you think may be the best match for your natural talents?

Linguistic **intelligence**—the ability to communicate through language (e.g., verbal skills in the areas of speaking, writing, listening, and reading)

Logical-mathematical **intelligence**—the ability to reason logically and succeed in tasks that involve mathematical problem solving (e.g., making logical arguments and following logical reasoning, or having the ability to work well with numbers and make quantitative calculations)

Spatial **intelligence**—the ability to visualize relationships among objects arranged in different spatial positions and the ability to perceive or create visual images (e.g., forming mental images such as three-dimensional objects; having the ability to detect detail in objects or drawings; being skilled at drawing, painting, sculpting, and graphic design; having a strong sense of direction and capacity to navigate unfamiliar places)

Musical **intelligence**—the ability to appreciate or create rhythmical and melodic sounds (e.g., playing, writing, and arranging music)

Interpersonal (social) **intelligence**—the ability to relate to others, to accurately identify others' needs, feelings, or emotional states of mind, and to effectively express emotions and feelings (e.g., interpersonal communication skills, ability to accurately "read" the feelings of others, and meet their emotional needs)

Intrapersonal (self) **intelligence**—the ability to introspect and understand one's own thoughts, feelings, and behavior (e.g., capacity for personal reflection, emotional self-awareness, and self-insight)

Bodily–kinesthetic (psychomotor) **intelligence**—the ability to use one's own body skillfully and learn through bodily sensations or movements; skilled at tasks involving physical coordination, ability to work well with hands, operate machinery, building models, assembling things, and using technology)

Naturalist **intelligence**—the ability to carefully observe and appreciate features of the natural environment; a keen awareness of nature or natural surroundings; the ability to understand causes and consequences of events occurring in the natural world

Existential **intelligence**—the ability to conceptualize phenomena and experiences that require one to go beyond sensory or physical evidence; to frame questions and examine issues involving the origin of the universe and human life; and to ponder the purpose of human existence

2. If you were to choose one country for a study-abroad or travel-study experience, what country would that be? In what way(s) would your experience in this country contribute to your personal growth, educational development, and career preparation?

3. In light of the ideas discussed in this chapter, how would you interpret or react to the following quotes?
   (a) "A liberal arts education is like the Mississippi River. It has many 'distributaries' that carry its water in all directions. It meanders—going west, north, and east—before it finds its ultimate direction [and] continues to meander even once it finds its direction, but this doesn't keep it from getting to its goal."

   —Dr. Richard Meadows, professor, Berea College, and author of "The Mississippi River vs. the Erie Canal: Mapping Out the Many Advantages of a Liberal Education"

   (b) "The mere presence of persons of other cultures and subcultures [on campus] is primarily a political achievement, not an intellectual or educational achievement. Real educational progress will be made when multiculturalism becomes inter-culturalism."

   —Patrick J. Hill, former provost, Evergreen State College

(c) "We do not learn from experience. We learn from reflecting on experience."
—John Dewey, influential philosopher, psychologist, and educational reformer

4. Following are different strategies for making use of your *elective* courses. Identify two of these strategies that appeal most to you and explain how you can begin to implement them.
    (a) To complete a minor
    (b) To help you find a career path
    (c) To strengthen your skills in areas that may appeal to future employers
    (d) To seek balance in your life and develop yourself as a whole person
    (e) To stretch beyond your familiar or customary learning style to experience different ways of learning and acquire new skills
    (f) To learn something you were always curious about, or that you know very little about

5. If you were to complete a college *minor* in addition to your college major, what would it be? In what way(s) do you think this minor would complement or augment your major?

Appendix:
Chapter Exercises

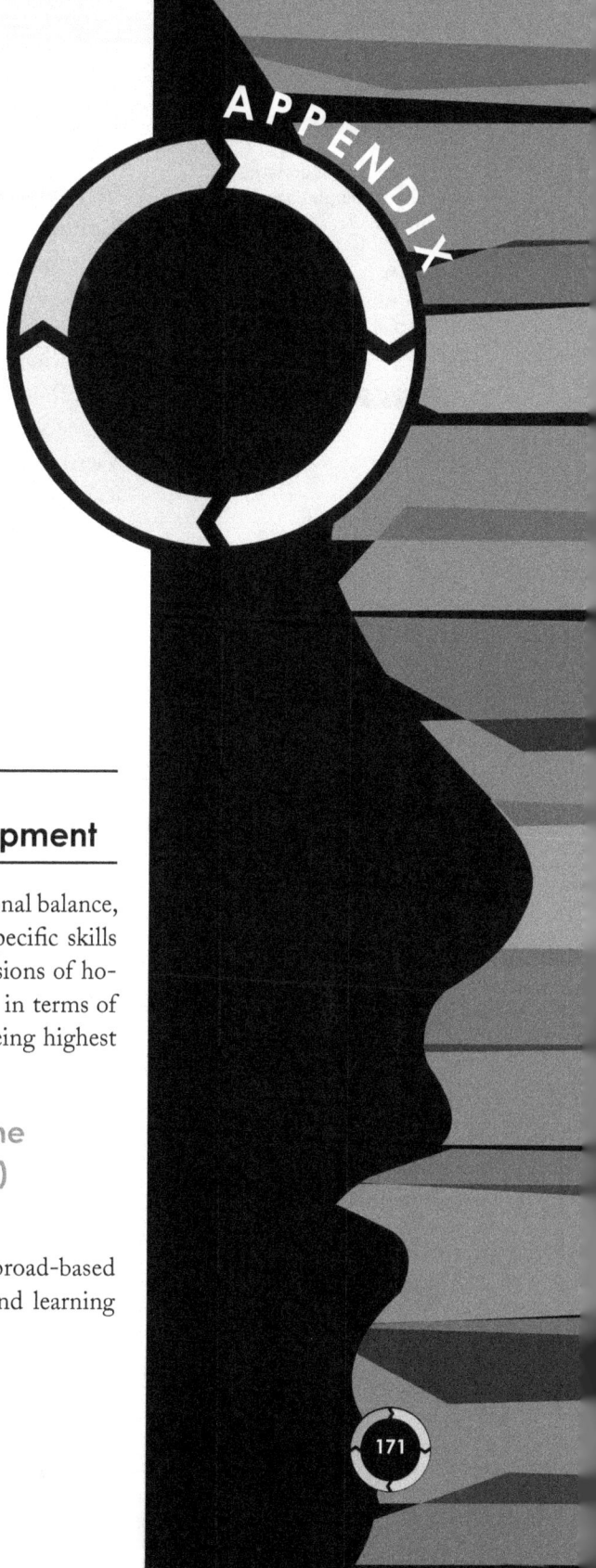

Chapter 1 Exercise

Self-Assessment of Holistic Development

Development of the whole self is essential for personal balance, wellness, and success. As you read through the specific skills and qualities associated with the following dimensions of holistic ("whole person") development, rate each one in terms of its *importance to you* on a scale of 1 to 5, with 5 being highest and 1 lowest.

Skills and Qualities Associated with the Dimensions of Holistic (Whole-Person) Development

1. **Intellectual development**—acquiring broad-based knowledge, learning how to learn deeply, and learning how to think critically

> "Intellectual growth should commence at birth and cease only at death."
>
> –Albert Einstein, Nobel Prize–winning physicist

Specific Skills and Qualities:

___ Becoming aware of your intellectual abilities, interests, and learning styles
___ Improving your focus of attention and concentration
___ Moving beyond memorizing factual information to learning at a deeper level
___ Improving your ability to retain knowledge (on a long-term basis)
___ Acquiring effective research skills for finding information from a variety of sources and systems
___ Viewing issues from multiple angles or viewpoints (psychological, social, political, economic, etc.) to gain a balanced, comprehensive perspective
___ Responding constructively to differing viewpoints or opposing arguments
___ Critically evaluating ideas in terms of their truth and value
___ Detecting and rejecting persuasion tactics that appeal to emotion rather than reason
___ Thinking creatively and innovatively

2. **Emotional development**—understanding, managing, and expressing emotions

Specific Skills and Qualities:

> "It's not stress that kills us, it is our reaction to it."
>
> —Hans Selye, Canadian endocrinologist and author of *Stress without Distress*

___ Dealing with personal emotions in an honest, nondefensive manner
___ Maintaining a healthy balance between emotional control and emotional expression
___ Responding with empathy and sensitivity to emotions experienced by others
___ Using effective stress-management strategies to control anxiety and reduce tension
___ Dealing effectively with depression
___ Dealing effectively with anger
___ Responding constructively to frustrations and setbacks
___ Dealing effectively with fear of failure and lack of self-confidence

___ Maintaining optimism and enthusiasm
___ Accepting feedback from others in a constructive, nondefensive manner

3. **Social development**—improving the quality and depth of interpersonal relationships

Specific Skills and Qualities:

___ Increasing social self-confidence
___ Improving listening and conversational skills
___ Overcoming shyness
___ Forming meaningful relationships
___ Learning how to resolve interpersonal conflicts effectively
___ Developing greater empathy for others
___ Relating effectively to others from different cultural backgrounds and lifestyles
___ Collaborating effectively with others when working in groups or teams
___ Becoming an effective community member
___ Strengthening leadership skills

> "Chi rispetta sara rippetato." ("Respect others and you will be respected.")
>
> –Italian proverb

4. **Ethical (character) development**—developing a clear value system for guiding personal decisions, making sound ethical judgments, and demonstrating consistency between your convictions (beliefs) and your commitments (actions)

Specific Skills and Qualities:

___ Gaining deeper awareness of personal values and ethical priorities
___ Making personal choices and life decisions based on a meaningful value system
___ Developing the capacity to think and act with personal integrity and authenticity
___ Resisting social pressure to act in ways that are inconsistent with your values

> "If you don't stand for something you will fall for anything."
>
> –Malcolm X, African American Muslim minister, public speaker, and human rights activist

___ Treating others in an ethically responsible manner
___ Exercising personal freedom responsibly without infringing on the rights of others
___ Increasing awareness of and commitment to human rights and social justice
___ Developing the courage to challenge or confront others who violate human rights and social justice
___ Using electronic technology in a civil and ethical manner
___ Becoming a more engaged and responsible citizen

5. **Physical development**—acquiring knowledge about the human body and how to apply that knowledge to prevent disease, preserve wellness, and promote peak performance

Specific Skills and Qualities:

> "A man too busy to take care of his health is like a mechanic too busy to take care of his tools."
>
> –Spanish proverb

___ Developing skills for self-monitoring your physical condition and state of health
___ Applying knowledge about exercise and fitness training to improve your physical and mental health
___ Understanding how sleep patterns affect your health and personal performance
___ Maintaining a healthy balance between work, recreation, and relaxation
___ Applying knowledge about nutrition to reduce risk of illness and promote peak performance
___ Becoming knowledgeable about nutritional imbalances and eating disorders
___ Developing a positive physical self-image
___ Increasing knowledge about the effects of drugs and how they affect physical and mental well-being
___ Gaining more knowledge about human sexuality and sexual diversity
___ Understanding how biological differences between the sexes affect male–female relationships

6. **Spiritual development**—devoting attention to the "big questions" about the meaning or purpose of life, the inevitability of death, and the origins of human life and the natural world

Specific Skills and Qualities:

____ Developing or refining your philosophy of life
____ Exploring the unknown or what cannot be completely understood scientifically
____ Appreciating the mysteries associated with the origin of the universe
____ Searching for the connection between the self and the larger world or cosmos
____ Searching for the mystical or supernatural—that which transcends the boundaries of the natural world
____ Examining questions relating to death and life after death
____ Exploring questions about the existence of a supreme being or higher power
____ Gaining knowledge about different approaches to spirituality and their underlying beliefs or assumptions
____ Understanding the difference and relationship between faith and reason
____ Becoming more aware and accepting of diverse religious beliefs and practices

> "We are not human beings having a spiritual experience. We are spiritual beings having a human experience."
>
> —Pierre Teilhard de Chardin, French philosopher, geologist, paleontologist, and Jesuit priest

7. **Vocational development**—exploring career options and pursuing a career path that is consistent with your interests, talents, and values

Specific Skills and Qualities:

____ Understanding the relationship between college majors and future careers
____ Using effective strategies for exploring and identifying potential careers
____ Identifying career options that are compatible with your personal interests, talents, needs, and values

> "Your work is to discover your work and then with all your heart to give yourself to it."
>
> —Hindu Siddhartha Prince Gautama Siddharta, a.k.a. Buddha, founder of the philosophy and religion of Buddhism

___ Acquiring work experience related to your vocational interests
___ Creating an effective resume or portfolio
___ Developing effective strategies for identifying personal references and sources for letters of recommendation
___ Implementing effective job-search strategies
___ Learning how to write persuasive letters of inquiry and letters of application for employment positions
___ Acquiring networking skills for connecting with potential employers
___ Developing strategies for performing successfully in job interviews

8. **Personal development**—developing a strong sense of personal identity, a coherent self-concept, and the ability to manage personal affairs and resources

Specific Skills and Qualities:

> "Remember, no one can make you feel inferior without your consent."
>
> —Eleanor Roosevelt, former United Nations diplomat and humanitarian

___ Developing a strong sense of identity and a coherent self-concept (i.e., answering the question: Who am I?)
___ Finding a sense of purpose and direction in life (i.e., answering the question: Who will I become?)
___ Developing greater self-respect and self-esteem
___ Increasing self-confidence
___ Developing self-efficacy—belief that the outcomes of your life are within your control and can be changed through personal initiative and effort
___ Strengthening skills for managing personal resources (e.g., time and money)
___ Becoming more independent, self-directed, and self-reliant
___ Setting realistic goals and priorities
___ Developing the self-motivation and self-discipline needed to reach long-term goals
___ Developing the resiliency to overcome obstacles and convert setbacks into comebacks

Humanity, Diversity, and the Liberal Arts: Foundation of a College Education

Add up your total score for each of the eight (8) areas of holistic development.
(a) Do your totals in each of the eight areas suggest that all aspects of self-development are about equally important to you and that you're striving to become a well-rounded person?
(b) If yes, why? If no, why not?

Based on your total score in all areas, what aspect(s) of self-development appear to be most and least important to you? How would you explain (or what do you think accounts for) this discrepancy?

Chapter 2 Exercise

Self-Assessment of Critical Thinking Characteristics

Critical thinking is not just an intellectual process, it's also a personal attribute. Listed here are attributes of critical thinkers accompanied by specific attributes associated with each characteristic. As you read the attributes under each of the general characteristics, place a checkmark (√) next to any attribute that you think is true of you now and an asterisk (*) next to any attribute you think you need to work on.

Attributes of Critical Thinkers

1. Tolerant and Accepting

___ Don't tune out ideas that conflict with their own
___ Keep emotions under control when someone criticizes their personal viewpoint
___ Feel comfortable discussing controversial issues
___ Try to find common ground with others holding opposing viewpoints

2. Inquisitive and Open Minded

___ Are eager to continue learning new things from different people and different experiences

___ Willing to seek out others who hold viewpoints different than their own.

___ Find differences of opinion and opposing viewpoints to be interesting and stimulating

___ Attempt to understand why people have come to adopt different conclusions and opposing viewpoints

3. Reflective and Tentative

___ Take time to think things through and consider all sides or perspectives of an issue before drawing conclusions, making choices, or reaching decisions

___ Give fair consideration to ideas that others may instantly disapprove of or find distasteful

___ Acknowledge the complexity, ambiguity, and uncertainty associated with certain issues, and are willing to say: "I need to give this more thought" or "I need more evidence before I can draw a conclusion"

___ Periodically reexamine their own viewpoints to see whether they should be maintained or changed

4. Honest and Courageous

___ Are willing to examine their views to determine if they stem from personal bias or defensiveness

___ Are willing to challenge ideas of others that are based on personal bias or prejudice

___ Are willing to express viewpoints that may not conform to those of the majority

___ Are willing to change previously held opinions and personal beliefs when they're contradicted by sound arguments or new evidence

Look back at the list and count the number of checkmarks and asterisks you placed in each of the four general areas:

	Checkmarks	Asterisks
Tolerant and Accepting:	___	___
Inquisitive and Open Minded:	___	___
Reflective and Tentative:	___	___
Honest and Courageous:	___	___

For which characteristic did you have (a) the most *checkmarks*, (b) the most *asterisks*?

What do you think accounts for this difference?

What could you do in college, by means of either curricular or co-curricular experiences, to strengthen your weakest area—that is, the attribute next to which you've placed the most asterisks?

Chapter 3 Exercise

Becoming Aware of Your Group Identities

We can be members of multiple groups at the same time and our membership in these overlapping groups can influence our personal development and identity. In the following figure, consider the shaded center circle to be yourself and the six non-shaded circles to be six different groups that you are a member of and that you think have influenced your development.

Fill in the non-shaded circles with the names of groups to which you think you belong that have had the most influence on your personal development and identity. You can use the diversity spectrum that appears in Chapter 3 to help you identify different groups to which you may belong. Don't feel you have to fill in all six circles. What is more important is to identify those groups that have had a significant influence on your development or identity.

After you identify these groups, take a moment to reflect on the following questions:

1. Which one of your groups has had the greatest influence on your personal development and identity? Why?

2. Have you ever felt limited or disadvantaged by being a member of any group(s)? Why?

3. Have you ever felt that you experienced advantages or privileges because of your membership in any group(s)? Why?

4. Reflecting on your responses to the above questions, which answer has the most personal significance or importance to you? Why?

Chapter 4 Exercise

Part A. Intercultural Interview

1. Identify a person on your campus from an ethnic or racial group that you've had little previous interaction. Ask that person for an interview, and during the interview, include the following questions.
   (a) What does "diversity" mean to you?

   (b) What prior experiences have affected your current viewpoints or attitudes about diversity?

   (c) What would you say have been the major influences and turning points in your life?

(d) Who would you cite as positive role models, heroes, or sources of inspiration in your life?

(e) What societal contributions made by your cultural group would you like others to be aware of and acknowledge?

(f) What do you hope will never again be said about your ethnic or racial group?

2. If you were the interviewee instead of the interviewer, how would you have answered the above questions?

3. What do you think accounts for the differences (and similarities) between your answers to the above questions and those provided by the person you interviewed?

Part B. Are You a Global Citizen?

Research on over 2,500 students from colleges across the country indicates that those students who consider themselves to be "global citizens" tend to agree with the following statements (46). Honestly assess yourself by placing a checkmark next to each statement that is true of you.

___ I am informed of current issues that impact international relations.
___ I understand how various cultures of this world interact socially.
___ I can discuss cultural differences from an informed perspective.
___ I am aware of how other cultures consider "fairness" differently from my own culture.
___ I intentionally involve people from many cultural backgrounds in my life.
___ I enjoy when my friends from other cultures teach me about our cultural differences.
___ People from other cultures tell me that I am successful at navigating their cultures.
___ I am open to people who strive to live lives very different from my own lifestyle.

___ I work for the rights of others.
___ I consciously behave in terms of making a difference.
___ I think of my life in terms of giving back to society.

Reflection Questions

1. Do you detect any pattern among the items you checked that may indicate a personal strength with respect to global citizenship? If yes, what is that strength and what have you done to develop it?

2. Do you detect any pattern among the items you didn't check that may indicate an aspect of global citizenship you need to strengthen? If yes, what could you do to strengthen it?

Chapter 5 Exercise

Part A. Developing an Education Plan for Making the Most of the Liberal Arts

Identify specific courses in your college catalog or university bulletin that fulfill general education requirements in different subject areas. Use the form below as a checklist to ensure that all key perspectives associated with the liberal arts are included and that there are no "blind spots" in your general education plan.

Broadening Social–Spatial Perspectives (See pages 14-19 for specific descriptions of these perspectives.)	Course Developing This Perspective (Read the course descriptions in your Catalog or Bulletin to identify a general education requirement that develops this perspective.)
Self	
Family	
Community	
Society	
Nation	
International	
Global	
Universe (Cosmos)	

Broadening Chronological Perspectives (See pages 20-21 for a detailed description of these perspectives.)	Course Developing This Perspective (Read the course descriptions in your Catalog to identify a general education requirement that develops this perspective.)
Historical	
Contemporary	
Futuristic	

Use the form below as a checklist for ensuring that your educational plan includes all key elements of holistic ("whole person") development.

Dimensions of Self (See page 124 for a detailed description of these dimensions of self-development.)	Course or Co-curricular Experience Developing This Dimension of Self (Consult your student handbook to identify a co-curricular experience that contributes to this dimension of self-development.)
Intellectual (Cognitive)	
Emotional	
Social	
Ethical	
Physical	
Spiritual	
Vocational	
Personal	

Part B. Developing an Educational Plan for Making the Most of Diversity

By infusing diversity into your college experience, you increase the power of the liberal arts by further broadening its multiple perspectives to adding to its repertoire of transferable, lifelong skills. Review your catalogue to identify diversity-related courses that you could take in each of the three key areas of college coursework: general education, your chose college major (or a major you're considering), and your elective courses. Use the following form to identify these courses.

Humanity, Diversity, and the Liberal Arts: Foundation of a College Education

| General Education Courses

See your college *catalogue* or *bulletin* for general education requirements. (If you completed the general education plan on page 183, see if any of those courses could also be listed here as addressing a dimension of diversity.) | Dimension of Diversity Developed by This Course

See the *Diversity Spectrum* on page 68 for a listing of different dimensions of diversity. Be sure to list at least one course that relates to cultural diversity within the United States (domestic diversity) and one that relates to cultural diversity across different nations (international diversity). |
|---|---|
| | |
| | |
| | |
| | |
| Requirements for Your College Major
(Or a Major that You Are Considering) | Dimension of Diversity Developed by This Course |
| | |
| | |
| | |
| | |
| Electives
(Not Required for General Education or Your Major) | Dimension of Diversity Developed by This Course |
| | |
| | |
| | |
| | |

APPENDIX: Chapter Exercises

References

1. AC Nielsen Research Services. (2000). *Employer satisfaction with graduate skills*. Department of Education, Training and Youth Affairs. Canberra: AGPS. Retrieved from http://www.dest.gov.au/ty/publications/employability_skills/final_report.pdf
2. Ackerman, J. M. (1993). The promise of writing to learn. *Written Communication, 10*(3), 334–370.
3. Acredolo, C., & O'Connor, J. (1991). On the difficulty of detecting cognitive uncertainty. *Human Development, 34*, 204–223.
4. Adelman, C. (2004). Global preparedness of pre-9/11 college graduates: What the U.S. longitudinal studies say. *Tertiary Education and Management, 10*, 243.
5. Allport. G. W. (1954). *The nature of prejudice*. Cambridge, MA: Addison-Wesley.
6. Allport, G. W. (1979). *The nature of prejudice* (3rd ed.). Reading, MA: Addison-Wesley.
7. American Association of University Women (AAUW). (2013). *The simple truth about the gender pay gap*. Washington, DC: Author.
8. American Council on Education. (2008). *Making the case for affirmative action*. Retrieved from http://www.acenet.edu/bookstore/descriptions/making_the_case/works/research.cfm
9. American Heart Association. (2006). *Fish, levels of mercury and omega-3 fatty acids*. Retrieved from http://americanheart.org/presenter.jthml?identifier=3013797
10. Amir, Y. (1969). Contact hypothesis in ethnic relations. *Psychological Bulletin, 71*, 319–342.
11. Amir, Y. (1976). The role of intergroup contact in change of prejudice and ethnic relations. In P. A. Katz (Ed.), *Towards the elimination of racism* (pp. 245–308). New York: Pergamon Press.
12. Anderson, M., & Fienberg, S. E. (2000). Race and ethnicity and the controversy over the U.S. census. *Current Sociology, 48*(3), 87–110.
13. Andres, L., & Wyn, J. (2010). *The making of a generation -- the children of the 1970s in adulthood.* Toronto, Buffalo, and London: University of Toronto Press.

14. Applebee, A. N. (1984). Writing and reasoning. *Review of Educational Research, 54*(4), 577–596.
15. Aronson, E., Wilson, T. D., & Akert, R. M. (2009). *Social psychology* (6th ed.). Upper Saddle River, NJ: Pearson/Prentice Hall.
16. Association of American Colleges & Universities. (2002). *Greater expectations: The commitment to quality as a nation goes to college.* Washington, DC: Author. Retrieved from http://www.greaterexpectaions.org/
17. Association of American Colleges & Universities (AAC&U). (2004). *Our students' best work*. Washington, DC: Author.
18. Association of American Colleges & Universities. (2007). *College learning for the new global century*. A report from the National Leadership Council for Liberal Education and America's Promise. Washington, DC: Author.
19. Astin, A. W. (1993). *What matters in college?* San Francisco: Jossey-Bass.
20. Astin, A. W., Vogelgesang, L. J., Ikeda, E. K., & Yee, J. A. (2000). *How service-learning affects students*. Los Angeles: Higher Education Research Institute, University of California.
21. Baer, J. M. (1993). *Creativity and divergent thinking*. Hillsdale, NJ: Erlbaum.
22. Banks, J. (1993). Approaches to multicultural curriculum reform. In J. Banks & C. Banks (Eds.), *Multicultural education: Issues and perspectives*. Boston: Allyn & Bacon.
23. Banks, J. A. (1995). Multicultural education and curriculum transformation. *The Journal of Negro Education, 64*(4), 390–400.
24. Banks, J. A., Cookson, P., Gay, G., Hawley, W., Irvine, J. J., Nieto, S., Schofield, J. W., & Stepan, W. (2001). Diversity within unity: Essential principles of teaching and learning in a multicultural society. *Phi Delta Kappan, 83*(3), 196–203.
25. Baron, R. S. (2005). So right it's wrong: Groupthink and the ubiquitous nature of polarized group decision making. *Advances in Experimental Social Psychology, 37*, 219–253.
26. Baron, R. A., Byrne, D., & Brauscombe, N. R. (2006). *Social psychology* (11th ed.). Boston: Pearson.
27. Bass, B. M., & Riggio, R. E. (2005). *Transformational leadership* (2nd ed.). Mahwah, NJ: Lawrence Erlbaum Associates.

28. Belenky, M. F., Clinchy, B., Goldberger, N. R., & Tarule, J. M. (1986). *Women's ways of knowing: The development of self, voice, and mind.* New York: Basic Books.
29. Bellah, R. N., Madsen, R., Sullivan, W. M., Swidler, A., & Tipton, S. M. (1985). *Habits of the heart: Individualism and commitment in American life.* Berkeley: University of California Press.
30. Bennis, W. (2009). *On becoming a leader.* Philadelphia: Basic Books.
31. Bensimon, E. M. (2007). The underestimated significance of practitioner knowledge in the scholarship on student success. *Review of Higher Education, 30*(4), 441–449.
32. Berg, T. G. (1983). Student development and liberal education. *NASPA Journal 21*(1), 9–16.
33. Berlin, I. (2004). American slavery in history and memory and the search for social justice. *Journal of American History, 90*(4), 1251–1268.
34. Bernstein, C. (1986). *Teaching about ethnic diversity.* Retrieved from http://www.ericdigests.org/pre-924/ethnic.htm
35. Bishop, S. (1986). Education for political freedom. *Liberal Education, 72*(4), 322–325.
36. Bishop, B. (2008). *The big sort: Why the clustering of like-minded America is tearing us apart.* New York: Houghton Mifflin.
37. Blair, I. V. (2002). The malleability of automatic stereotypes and prejudice. *Personality and Social Psychology Review, 6*(3), 242–261.
38. Bligh, D. A. (2000). *What's the use of lectures.* San Francisco: Jossey-Bass.
39. Bodian, S. (2006). *Meditation for dummies* (2nd ed.). Indianapolis, IN: Wiley Publishing.
40. Bok, D. (2006). *Our underachieving colleges.* Princeton, NJ: Princeton University Press.
41. Bolles, R. N. (1998). *The new quick job-hunting map.* Toronto, Ontario, Canada: Ten Speed Press.
42. Boren D. (2008). *A letter to America.* Norman, OK: University of Oklahoma Press.
43. Bourdieu, P. (1986). The forms of capital. In J. Richardson (Ed.), *Handbook of theory and research for the social psychology of education* (pp. 241–258). Westport, CT: Greenwood Press.

44. Bowen, H. R. (1977). *Investment in learning: The individual and social value of American higher education.* San Francisco: Jossey-Bass.
45. Bowen, H. R. (1997). *Investment in learning: The individual and social value of American higher education* (2nd ed.). Baltimore: The Johns Hopkins Press.
46. Braskamp, L. A. (2008). Developing global citizens. *Journal of College and Character, 10*(1), 1–5.
47. Bridgeman, B. (2003). *Psychology and evolution: The origins of mind.* Thousand Oaks, CA: Sage.
48. Bronfenbrenner, U. (Ed.) (2005). *Making human beings human: Bioecological perspectives on human development.* Thousand Oaks, CA: Sage.
49. Brookfield, S. D. (1987). *Developing critical thinkers.* San Francisco: Jossey-Bass.
50. Brookings Institute. (2008). *Demographic keys to the 2008 election.* Washington, DC: Brookings Institute. Retrieved from www.brookings.edu/~/media/Files/events/2008/1020_demographic/20081020_demographics.pdf
51. Brooks, K. (2009). *You majored in what? Mapping your path from chaos to career.* New York: Penguin.
52. Brooks, K. (2013). Marketing and using your foreign language skills at work. *Career transitions: Turning chaos into careers.* Retrieved from http://www.psychologytoday.com/blog/career-transitions/201302/marketing-and-using-your-foreign-language-skills-work
53. Brown, D. (2003). *Career information, career counseling, and career development* (8th ed.). Boston: Allyn & Bacon.
54. Brown, R., & Hewstone, M. (2005). An integrative theory of intergroup contact. In M. P. Zanna (Ed.), *Advances in experimental social psychology* (vol. 37, pp. 255–343). San Diego: Elsevier Academic Press.
55. Brown, T. D., Dane, F. C., & Durham, M. D. (1998). Perception of race and ethnicity. *Journal of Social Behavior and Personality, 13*(2), 295–306.
56. Brown, K. T., Brown, T. N., Jackson, J. S., Sellers, R. M., & Manuel, W. J. (2003). Teammates on and off the field? Contact with Black teammates and the racial attitudes of White student athletes. *Journal of Applied Social Psychology, 33,* 1379–1403.

57. Brown, J. S., Collins, A., & Duguid, P. (1989). Situated cognition and the culture of learning. *Educational Researcher, 18*, 32–42.
58. Bruffee, K. A. (1993). *Collaborative learning: Higher education, interdependence, and the authority of knowledge.* Baltimore: Johns Hopkins University Press.
59. Bureau of Labor Statistics. (2012). *Highlights of women's earnings in 2011.* U.S. Department of Labor, U.S. Bureau of Labor Statistics, Report 1038. Retrieved from http://www.bls.gov/cps/cpswom2011.pdf
60. Business-Higher Education Forum. (1999). *Spanning the chasm: A blueprint for action.* Washington, DC: Author.
61. Business-Higher Education Forum. (2002). *Investing in people: Developing all of America's talent on campus and in the workplace.* Washington, DC: Author.
62. Canuto, M. A., & Yaeger, J. (Eds.) (2000). *The archaeology of communities.* New York: Routledge.
63. Caplan, P. J., & Caplan, J. B. (1994). *Thinking critically about research on sex and gender.* New York: Harper Collins College Publishers.
64. Carlson, J. S., Burn, B. B., Useem, J., & Yachimowicz, D. (1990). *Study abroad: The experience of American undergraduates.* New York: Greenwood Press.
65. Carnevale, A. P., Strohl, J., & Melton, M. (2011). Selected findings from *What's worth it? The economic value of college majors.* Washington, DC: U.S. Department of Education, National Center for Educational Statistics.
Retrieved from http://nces.ed.gov/pibs2011/2011236.pdf
66. Center for Postsecondary and Economic Success. (2011). *Yesterday's nontraditional student is today's traditional student.* Retrieved from www.clasp.org/admin/site/.../Nontraditional-Students-Facts-2011.pdf
67. Chang, M. J., Denson, N., Saenz, V., & Misa, K. (2006). The educational benefits of sustaining cross-racial interaction among undergraduates. *Journal of Higher Education, 77*(3), 430–455.
68. Chatman, S. (2008). *Does diversity matter in the education process?* Research & Occasional Paper Series: CSHE.5.08 Berkeley, CA:

Center for Studies in Higher Education (CSHE), University of California, Berkeley. Retrieved from cshe.berkeley.edu/publications/docs/ROPS.Chatman.Exploring.2.5.08.pdf

69. Chronicle of Higher Education. (2003, August 30). *Almanac 2003–04, 49*(1). Washington, DC: Author.
70. Cianciotto, J. (2005). *Hispanic and Latino same-sex couple households in the United States: A report from the 2000 Census*. New York: The National Gay and Lesbian Task Force Policy Institute and the National Latino/a Coalition for Justice.
71. College Board. (2008). *Coming to our senses: Education and the American future. Report of the Commission on Access, Admissions and Success in Higher Education.* Retrieved from www.http:advocacy.collegeboard.org/.../coming-to-our-senses-college-board-2
72. College Board. (2013). *Education pays 2013: The benefits of higher education for individuals and society.* Washington, DC: Author.
73. Collins, A., Brown, J. S., & Newman, S. E. (1989). Cognitive apprenticeship: Teaching the crafts of reading, writing, and mathematics. In L. B. Resnick (Ed.), *Knowing, learning, and instruction: Essays in honor of Robert Glaser* (pp. 453–494). Hillsdale, NJ: Lawrence Erlbaum Associates.
74. Colombo, G., Cullen, R., & Lisle, B. (2010). *Rereading America: Cultural contexts for critical thinking and writing* (8th ed.). Boston: Bedford Books of St. Martin's Press.
75. Conference Board of Canada. (2000). *Employability skills 2000+*. Retrieved from www.conferenceboard.ca/Libraries/educ_public/esp2000.sflb
76. Conley, D. T. (2005). *College knowledge: What it really takes for students to succeed and what we can do to get them ready.* San Francisco: Jossey-Bass.
77. Cook, S. W. (1984). Cooperative interaction in multiethnic contexts. In N. B. Miller and M. B. Brewer (Eds.), *Groups in contact: The psychology of desegregation.* New York: Academic Press.
78. Covey, S. R. (1990). *Seven habits of highly effective people* (2nd ed.). New York: Fireside.
79. Covey, S. R., Merrill, A. R., & Merrill, R. R. (1996). *First things first: To live, to love, to learn, to leave a legacy.* New York: Fireside.

80. Cronon, W. (1998). "Only connect": The goals of a liberal education. *The American Scholar, 67(4),* 73–80.
81. Cross, K. P. (1982). Thirty years passed: Trends in general education. In B. L. Johnson (Ed.), *General education in two-year colleges* (pp. 11–20). San Francisco: Jossey-Bass.
82. Cummings, M. C. (2002). *Democracy under pressure* (9th ed.). Belmont, CA: Wadsworth.
83. Curren, R. (Ed.) (2007). *Philosophy of education: An anthology.* Oxford: Blackwell.
84. Cuseo, J. B. (1996). *Cooperative learning: A pedagogy for addressing contemporary challenges and critical issues in higher education.* Stillwater, OK: New Forums Press.
85. Cuseo, J. B. (1998). Objectives and benefits of senior year programs. In J. N. Gardner & G. Van der Veer (Eds.), *The senior year experience: Facilitating integration, reflection, closure, and transition* (pp. 21–36). San Francisco: Jossey-Bass.
86. Cuseo, J. B. (2002). *Igniting student involvement, peer interaction, and teamwork: A taxonomy of specific cooperative learning structures and collaborative learning strategies.* Stillwater, OK: New Forums Press.
87. Cuseo, J. B. (2005). "Decided," "undecided," and "in transition": Implications for academic advisement, career counseling, and student retention. In R. S. Feldman (Ed.), *Improving the first year of college: Research and practice* (pp. 27–50). Mahwah, NJ: Lawrence Erlbaum.
88. Cuseo, J. B., Thompson, A., Campagna, M., & Fecas, V. S. (2013). *Thriving in college and beyond: Research-based strategies for academic success and personal development* (3rd ed.). Dubuque, IA: Kendall Hunt.
89. Daly, W. T. (1992, July/August). The academy, the economy, and the liberal arts. *Academe,* pp. 10–12.
90. Daly, H. E. (1999). *Ecological economics and the ecology of economics.* Cheltenham, UK: Edward Elgar Publishing.
91. Dee, T. (2004). Are there civic returns to education? *Journal of Public Economics, 88,* 1697–1720.
92. DeNavas-Walt, C., Proctor, B. D., & Smith, J. C. (2013). *Income, poverty, and health insurance coverage in the United States, 2012.* U.S. Census Bureau, Current Population Reports, P60-245, Washington, DC: U.S. Government Printing Office.

93. Donald, J. G. (2002). *Learning to think: Disciplinary perspectives.* San Francisco: Jossey-Bass.
94. Dovidio, J. F., Eller, A., & Hewstone, M. (2011). Improving intergroup relations through direct, extended and other forms of indirect contact. *Group Processes & Intergroup Relations, 14,* 147–160.
95. Dryden, G., & Vos, J. (1999). *The learning revolution: To change the way the world learns.* Torrance, CA and Auckland, New Zealand: The Learning Web.
96. Dupuy, G. M., & Vance, R. M. (1996, October). *Launching your career: A transition module for seniors.* Paper presented at the Second National Conference on Students in Transition, San Antonio, Texas.
97. Eble, K. E. (1966). *A perfect education.* New York: Macmillan.
98. Education Commission of the States. (1995). *Making quality count in undergraduate education.* Denver, CO: ECS Distribution Center.
99. Elbow, P. (1973). *Writing without teachers.* New York: Oxford University Press.
100. Encrenaz, T., Bibring, J. P., Blanc M., Barucci, M. A., Roques, F., & Zarka, P. (2004). *The solar system.* Berlin, Germany: Springer.
101. Erickson, B. L., Peters, C. B., & Strommer, D. W. (2006). *Teaching first-year college students.* San Francisco: Jossey-Bass.
102. Family Care Foundation. (1997-2012). *If the world were a village of 100 people.* Retrieved from www.familycare.org/.../if-the-world-were-a-village-of-100-people/
103. Feagin, J., & Feagin, C. (2007). *Racial and ethnic relations* (3rd ed.). Upper Saddle River, NJ: Prentice Hall.
104. Feldman, K. A., & Newcomb, T. M. (1994). *The impact of college on students.* New Brunswick, NJ: Transaction Publishers. (Originally published in 1969 by Jossey-Bass.)
105. Feskens, E. J., & Kromhout, D. (1993). Epidemiologic studies on Eskimos and fish intake. *Annals of the New York Academy of Science, 683,* 9–15.
106. Fidelibus, S. (2011, June 17). *Media coverage misunderstands the value of a college education.* Poynter. Retrieved from http://www.poynter.org/lates-news/making-sense-of-news/136205/media-coverage-misunderstands-the-value-of-a-college-education/

107. Figler, H., & Bolles, R. N. (2007). *The career counselor's handbook.* Berkeley, CA: Ten Speed Press.
108. Fixman, C. S. (1990). The foreign language needs of U.S.-based corporations. *Annals of the American Academy of Political and Social Science, 511,* 25–46.
109. Fogel, R. W. (1989). *Without consent or contract: The rise and fall of American slavery.* New York: W. W. Norton.
110. Franklin, K. F. (2002. Conversations with Metropolitan University first-year students. *Journal of the First-Year Experience and Students in Transition, 14*(2), 57–88.
111. Friedman, T. L. (2005). *The world is flat: A brief history of the twenty-first century.* New York: Farrar, Straus & Giroux.
112. Gamson, Z. F. (1984). *Liberating education.* San Francisco: Jossey-Bass.
113. Gardiner, L. F. (2005). Transforming the environment for learning: A crisis of quality. *To Improve the Academy, 23,* 3–23.
114. Gardner, H. (1999). *Intelligence reframed: Multiple intelligences for the twenty-first century.* New York: Basic Books.
115. Gardner, H. (2006). *Five minds for the future.* Cambridge, MA: Harvard Business School Press.
116. Ginsberg, M. B., & Wlodkowski, R. J. (2009). *Diversity & motivation* (2nd ed.). San Francisco: Jossey-Bass.
117. Glassman, J. K. (2000, June 9). The technology revolution: Road to freedom or road to serfdom? *Heritage Lectures,* No. 668. Washington, DC: The Heritage Foundation.
118. Goleman, D. (1992, Oct. 27). Voters assailed by unfair persuasion. *The New York Times,* pp. C1–C3.
119. Goleman, D. (1995). *Emotional intelligence: Why it can matter more than IQ.* New York: Random House.
120. Goodland, R. (2002). Sustainability: Human, social, economic, and environmental. In T. Munn (Ed.), *Encyclopedia of global environmental change* (pp. 488-489). Hoboken, NJ: Wiley.
121. Gordon, V. N., & Steele, G. E. (2003). Undecided first-year students: A 25-year longitudinal study. *Journal of the First-Year Experience and Students in Transition, 15*(1), 19–38.
122. Gorksi, P. (1995). *A course in race and ethnicity: Language of closet racism.* Retrieved from http://curry.edschool.virginia.edu/go/multicultural/langofracism2.html

123. Gorksi, P. (2009). What we're teaching teachers: An analysis of multicultural teacher education coursework syllabi. *Teaching and Teacher Education, 25*(2), 309–318.
124. Goslin, A. (2007–2008). Bored? *Scientific American Mind, 18*(6), 20–27.
125. Grey, W. (1993). Anthropocentrism and deep ecology. *Australasian Journal of Philosophy, 71*, 463–475
126. Grieco, E. M., Acosta, Y. D., de la Cruz, G. P., Gambino, C., Gryn, T., Larsen, L. J., & Walters, N. P. (2012). *The foreign-born population in the United States: 2010.* U.S. Census Bureau. American Community Survey. Retrieved from http://www.census.gov/prod/2012pubs/acs-19.pdf
127. Gurin, P. (1999, Spring). New research on the benefits of diversity in college and beyond: An empirical analysis. *Diversity Digest.* Retrieved from http://www.diversityweb.org/Digest/Sp99/benefits.html
128. Gutmann, A. (1999). *Democratic education.* Princeton, NJ: Princeton University Press.
129. Hamilton, W. (2011, December 29). College still worth it, study says. *Los Angeles Times*, p. B2.
130. Hamilton, W. (2014, May 8). 83% of college grads lack a job. *Los Angeles Times*, p. B2.
131. Hamilton, W. (2014, June 25). College still good bet, study says. *Los Angeles Times*, p. B4.
132. Hanuskek, E. A., Schwerdt, G., Wiederhold, S., & Woessmann, L. (2013). *Return to skills around the world: Evidence from PIAAC.* NBER Working Paper No. 19762. Retrieved from http://www.nber.org/papers/w19762
133. Harris, R. (2001). *On the purpose of a liberal arts education.* Retrieved from http://www.virtualsalt.com/libarted.htm
134. Hart Research Associates. (2006). *How should college prepare students to succeed in today's global economy?* Washington, DC: American Association of Colleges & Universities.
135. Hart Research Associates. (2009). *Raising the bar: Employers' views on college learning in the wake of the economic downturn.* Washington, DC: Author. Retrieved from http://www.aacu.org/leap/documents/2009_EmployerSurvey.pdf

136. Hart Research Associates. (2013). *It takes more than a major: Employer priorities for college learning and student success.* Washington, DC: Author.
137. Hazlehurst, J. (2010, August. 27). Learning a foreign language: Now you're talking. *The Guardian.* Retrieved from http://www.guardian.co.uk/money/2010/aug/28/learning-foreign-language-boost-career
138. Heath, H. (1976). What the enduring effects of higher education tell us about liberal education. *Journal of Higher Education, 47,* 173–190.
139. Heath, H. (1977). *Maturity and competence: A transcultural view.* New York: Halsted Press.
140. Herman, R. E. (2000). Liberal arts: The key to the future. *USA Today Magazine* (November), *129,* p. 34.
141. Hersh, R. (1997). Intentions and perceptions: A national survey of public attitudes toward liberal arts education. *Change, 29*(2), 16–23.
142. Higher Education Institute (HERI). (2009). *The American college teacher: National norms for 2007-2008.* Los Angeles: HERI, University of California.
143. Hugenberg, K., & Bodenhausen, G. V. (2003). Facing prejudice: Implicit prejudice and the perception of facial threat. *Psychological Science, 14,* 640–643.
144. Humphreys, D. (2006). *Making the case for liberal education: Responding to challenges.* Washington, DC: AAC&U. Retrieved from http://www.aacu.org/leap/documents/LEAP_Makingthe Case_Final.pdf
145. IES Abroad News. (2002). *Study abroad: A lifetime of benefits.* Retrieved from www.iesabroad.org/study-abroad/news/study-abroad-lifetime-benefits
146. Indiana University. (2004). *Selling your liberal arts degree to employers.* Bloomington, IN: Indiana University, Arts and Sciences Placement Office. Retrieved from http://www.indiana.edu/~career/fulltime/selling_liberal_arts.html
147. Inoue, Y. (2005, April). *Critical thinking and diversity experiences: A connection.* Paper presented at the Annual Meeting of the American Educational Research Association, Montreal, Canada.

148. Intergovernmental Council on Climate Change. (2013). *Climate change 2013: The physical science basis.* Working Group I Contribution to the Fifth Assessment Report of the Intergovernmental Council on Climate Change. Switzerland: Intergovernmental Panel on Climate Change. Retrieved from http://www.climatechange2013.org/images/uploads/WGI_AR5_SPM_brochure.pdf

149. International Wellness Directory. (2009). *The history of quackery.* Retrieved from http://www.mnwelldir.org/docs/history/quackery.htm

150. Jablonski, N. G., & Chaplin, G. (2002). Skin deep. *Scientific American* (October), 75–81.

151. Janis, I. L. (1982). *Groupthink: Psychological studies of policy decisions and fiascoes* (2nd ed.). Boston: Houghton Mifflin.

152. Johnson, D., Johnson, R., & Smith, K. (1998). Cooperative learning returns to college: What evidence is there that it works? *Change, 30,* 26–35.

153. Joint Science Academies Statement. (2005). *Global response to climate change.* Retrieved from http://nationalacademies.org/onpi/06072005.pdf

154. Judd, C. M., Ryan, C. S., & Parke, B. (1991). Accuracy in the judgment of in-group and out-group variability. *Journal of Personality and Social Psychology, 61,* 366–379.

155. Katz, S. N. (2008, May 23). Taking the true measure of liberal education. *Chronicle of Higher Education,* p. 32.

156. Katz, J., & Henry, M. (1993). *Turning professors into teachers: A new approach to faculty development and student learning.* Phoenix: American Council on Education and Oryx Press.

157. Kaufman, J. C., & Baer, J. (2002). Could Steven Spielberg manage the Yankees? Creative thinking in different domains. *Korean Journal of Thinking and Problem Solving, 12*(2), 5–14.

158. Kaufmann, N. L., Martin, J. M., & Weaver, H. D. (1992). *Students abroad: Strangers at home: Education for a global society.* Yarmouth, ME: Intercultural Press.

159. Kearns, D. (1989). Getting schools back on track. *Newsweek* (November), 8–9.

160. Kegan, R. (1994). *In over our heads: The mental demands of modern life.* Cambridge, MA: Harvard University Press.

161. Kelly, K. (1994). *Out of control: The new biology of machines, social systems, and the economic world.* Reading, MA: Addison-Wesley.
162. Khoshaba, D. M., & Maddi, S. R. (1999–2004). *HardiTraining: Managing stressful change.* Newport Beach, CA: The Hardiness Institute.
163. Kim, Y. M. (2011). *Minorities in higher education: Twenty-fourth status report, 2011 supplement.* Washington, DC: American Council on Education.
164. Kimball, B. (1986). *Orators and philosophers: A history of the idea of liberal arts.* New York: Teachers College Press.
165. King, P. N., Brown, M. K., Lindsay, N. K., & Vanhencke, J. R. (2007, Sep/Oct). Liberal arts student learning outcomes: An integrated approach. *About Campus,* 2–9.
166. Kitchener, K., Wood, P., & Jensen, L. (2000, August). *Curricular, co-curricular, and institutional influence on real-world problem-solving.* Paper presented at the annual meeting of the American Psychological Association, Boston.
167. Kluger, J. (2013). The pursuit of happiness. *Time, 21*(3), 24–40.
168. Knoll, A. H. (2003). *Life on a young planet: The first three billion years of evolution on earth.* Princeton, NJ: Princeton University Press.
169. Kochlar, R., Fry, R., & Taylor, P. (2011, July). Wealth gaps rise to record highs between Whites, Blacks, Hispanics, twenty-to-one. *Pew Research Social and Demographics Trends.* Retrieved from http://www.pewsocialtrends.org
170. Komives, S., & Wagner, W. (2009). *Leadership for a better world: Understanding the social change model of leadership development*: San Francisco: Jossey-Bass
171. Kuh, G. D. (1995). The other curriculum: Out-of-class experiences associated with student learning and personal development. *Journal of Higher Education, 66*(2), 123–153.
172. Kuh, G. D., Douglas, K. B., Lund, J. P., & Ramin-Gyurnek, J. (1994). *Student learning outside the classroom: Transcending artificial boundaries.* ASHE-ERIC Higher Education Report, No. 8. Washington, DC: George Washington University, School of Education and Human Development.
173. Kurfiss, J. G. (1988). *Critical thinking: theory, research, practice, and possibilities.* ASHE-ERIC, Report No. 2. Washington, DC: Association for the Study of Higher Education.

174. Lancaster, L., & Stillman, D. (2002). *When generations collide.* New York: Harper Collins.
175. Latané, B., Liu, J. H., Nowak, A., Bonevento, N., & Zheng, L. (1995). Distance matters: Physical space and social impact. *Personality and Social Psychology Bulletin, 21,* 795–805.
176. LeBaron, M. (2003). *Bridging cultural conflicts: New approaches for a changing world.* San Francisco: Jossey-Bass.
177. Leung, A. K., Maddux, W. W., Galinsky, A. D., & Chie-yue, C. (2008). Multicultural experience enhances creativity: The when and how. *American Psychologist, 63*(3), 169–181.
178. Levine, L. W. (1996). *The opening of the American mind: Canons, culture, and history.* Boston: Beacon Press.
179. Lewis, M., Paul, G. F., & Fennig, C. D. (Eds.). (2014). *Ethnologue: Languages of the world* (17th ed.). Dallas: SIL International. Online version available at: http://www.ethnologue.com
180. Light, R. J. (2001). *Making the most of college: Students speak their minds.* Cambridge, MA: Harvard University Press.
181. Lock, R. D. (2004). *Taking charge of your career direction* (5th ed.). Belmont, CA: Brooks Cole.
182. *Los Angeles Times* (2004, April 4).
183. Love, P., & Love, A. G. (1995). *Enhancing student learning: Intellectual, social, and emotional integration.* ASHE-ERIC Higher Education Report No. 4. Washington, DC: The George Washington University. Graduate School of Education and Human Development.
184. Luhman, R. (2007). *The sociological outlook.* Lanham, MD: Rowman & Littlefield.
185. Mackes, M. (2003). Employers describe perfect job candidate. *NACEWeb Press Releases.* Retrieved from http://www.naceweb.org/press
186. Maddux, W. W., & Galinsky, A. (2009). Cultural borders and mental barriers: The relationship between living abroad and creativity. *Journal of Personality & Social Psychology, 96*(5), 1047–1061.
187. Magolda, M. B. B. (1992). *Knowing and reasoning in college.* San Francisco: Jossey-Bass.
188. McIntosh, P. (1989). White privilege: Unpacking the invisible knapsack. *Peace and Freedom* (July/August), 9–10.

189. McIntosh, P. (2000). Interactive phases of personal and curricular re-vision with regard to race. In G. Shin & P. Gorski (Eds.), *Multicultural resource series: Professional development for educators*. Washington, DC: National Education Association.

190. Mendez, F., Krahn, T., Schrack, B., Krahn, A. M., Veeramah, K., Woerner, A., Fomine, F. L. M., Bradman, N., Thomas, M., Karafet, T., & Hammer, M. (2013). An African American paternal lineage adds an extremely ancient root to the human Y chromosome phylogenetic tree. *The American Journal of Human Genetics, 92*, 454–459.

191. Meredith, M. (2011). *Born in Africa: The quest for the origins of human life*. New York: Public Affairs

192. Millard, B. (2004, November 7). *A purpose-based approach to navigating college transitions*. Preconference workshop presented at the Eleventh National Conference on Students in Transition, Nashville, Tennessee.

193. Miller, G. (1988). *The meaning of general education*. New York: Teachers College Press.

194. Milton, O. (1982). *Will that be on the final?* Springfield, IL: Charles C. Thomas.

195. Miville, M. L., Molla, B., & Sedlacek, W. E. (1992). Attitudes of tolerance for diversity among college students. *Journal of the Freshman Year Experience, 4*(1), 95–110.

196. Moe, M. T., & Blodgett, H. (2003). *The knowledge web: People power—fuel for the new economy 2000*. Washington, DC: National Center for Educational Statistics.

197. Molnar, S. (1991). *Human variation: Race, type, and ethnic groups* (3rd ed.). Englewood Cliffs, NJ: Prentice-Hall.

198. Morse, S. (1989). *Renewing civic capacity: Preparing college students for service and citizenship*. Washington, DC: School of Education and Human Development, George Washington University.

199. Myers, D. G. (1993). *The pursuit of happiness: Who is happy—and why?* New York: Morrow.

200. Myers, N. (1997). The rich diversity of biodiversity issues. In M. L. Reaka-Kudla, D. E. Wilson, & E. O. Wilson (Eds.), *Biological diversity II: Understanding and protecting our biological resources* (pp. 125-134). National Academic of Sciences, Washington, DC: Joseph Henry Press.

201. Myers, D. G., & Lamm, H. (1975). The polarizing effect of group discussion. *American Scientist, 63*(3), 297–303.
202. Nagda, B. R., Gurin, P., & Johnson, S. M. (2005). Living, doing and thinking diversity: How does pre-college diversity experience affect first-year students' engagement with college diversity? In R. S. Feldman (Ed.), *Improving the first year of college: Research and practice* (pp. 73–110). Mahwah, NJ: Lawrence Erlbaum Associates.
203. Nagda, B. R., Gurin, P., & Lopez, G. E. (2003). Transformative pedagogy for democracy and social justice. *Race, Ethnicity, and Education, 6*(2), 165–191.
204. Naisbitt, J. (1982). *Megatrends: Ten new directions transforming our lives*. New York: Warner Books.
205. Nathan, R. (2005). *My freshman year: What a professor learned by becoming a student*. London: Penguin.
206. National Association of Colleges and Employers (NACE). (2003). *Job outlook 2003 survey*. Bethlehem, PA: Author.
207. National Association of Colleges & Employers. (2007). *Developing the diverse college-educated work force*. Retrieved from www.naceweb.org/Journal/2007october/Diverse_Work_Force/?...
208. National Association of Colleges and Employers. (2010). *2009 experiential education survey*. Bethlehem, PA: Author.
209. National Center for Education Statistics. (2011). *Digest of education statistics, table 237. Total fall enrollment in degree-granting institutions, by level of student, sex, attendance status, and race/ethnicity: Selected years, 1976 through 2010*. Alexandria, VA: U.S. Department of Education. Retrieved from http://neces.ed/gov/programs/digest/d11/tables/dt11_237.asp
210. National Center for Education Statistics. (2014). *Fast facts: Most popular majors*. Washington, DC: U.S. Department of Education. Retrieved from http://nces.ed.gov/fastfacts/display.asp?id=37
211. National Committee on Pay Equity. (2008). *The wage gap over time: In real dollars, women see a continuing gap*. Retrieved from http:www.pay-equity.org/info-time.html
212. National Council for the Social Sciences (NCSS). (1991). *Curriculum guidelines for multicultural education*. Prepared by the NCSS Task Force on Ethnic Studies Curriculum Guidelines. Retrieved from www.socialstudies.org/positions/multicultural

213. National Resources Defense Council. (2005). *Global warming: A summary of recent findings on the changing global climate.* Retrieved from http://www.nrdc.org/global/Warming/fgwscience.asp
214. National Resources Defense Council. (2012). *Global warming: An introduction to climate change.* Retrieved from http://www.nrdc.org/globalwarming/
215. National Survey of Voters. (1998). *Autumn overview report conducted by DYG Inc.* Retrieved from htttp://www.diversityweb.org/research_and_trends/research_evaluation_impact_/campus_community_connections/ national_poll.cfm
216. Nemko, M. (1988). *How to get an ivy league education at a state university.* New York: Avon Books.
217. Newman, J. H. (1852/1907). *The idea of a university.* New York: Longmans, Green, & Co.
218. Nhan, D. (2012). Census: Minorities constitute 37 percent of U.S. population. *National Journal: The Next America-Demographics 2012.* Retrieved from http://www.nationaljournal.com/thenextamerica/demographics/census-minorities-constitute-37-percent-of-u-s-population-20120517
219. Nicholas, R. W. (1991). Cultures in the curriculum. *Liberal Education, 77*(3), 16–21.
220. Niles, S. G., & Harris-Bowlsbey, J. (2002). *Career development interventions in the twenty-first century.* Upper Saddle River, NJ: Pearson Education.
221. Norse, E. A. (1990). *The wilderness society.* Washington, DC: Island Press.
222. Novinger, T. (2001). *Intercultural communication: A practical guide.* Austin, TX: University of Texas Press.
223. Nussbaum, M. C. (1997). *Cultivating humanity: A classical defense of reform in liberal education.* Cambridge, MA: Harvard University Press.
224. Obama, B. (2006). *The audacity of hope: Thoughts on reclaiming the American dream.* New York: Three Rivers Press.
225. Office of Research. (1994). *What employers expect of college graduates: International knowledge and second language skills.* Washington, DC: Office of Educational Research and Improvement (OERI), U.S. Department of Education.

226. Ogbu, J. (1990). Overcoming racial barriers to equal access. In J. Goodland & P. Keating (Eds.), *Access to knowledge: An agenda for our nation's schools* (pp. 85–104). New York: Elsivier/North-Holland.
227. Oller, D. K. (1981). Infant vocalizations: Exploration and reflectivity. In R. E. Stark (Ed.), *Language behavior in infancy and early childhood* (pp. 85–104). New York: Elsevier/North-Holland.
228. Olson, L. (2007). What does "ready" mean? *Education Week, 40,* 7–12.
229. Palmer, B. (2000, Winter). The impact of diversity courses: Research from Pennsylvania State University. *Diversity Digest.* Retrieved from http://www.diversityweb.org/Digest/W00/research.html
230. Pascarella, E. T. (2001, Nov/Dec). Cognitive growth in college: Surprising and reassuring findings from The National Study of Student Learning. *Change,* 21–27.
231. Pascarella, E., & Terenzini, P. (1991). *How college affects students: Findings and insights from twenty years of research.* San Francisco: Jossey-Bass.
232. Pascarella, E. T., & Terenzini, P. T. (2005). *How college affects students: A third decade of research* (vol. 2). San Francisco: Jossey-Bass.
233. Pascarella, E., Palmer, B., Moye, M., & Pierson, C. (2001). Do diversity experiences influence the development of critical thinking? *Journal of College Student Development, 42,* 257–291.
234. Paul, R. W., & Elder, L. (2011). *Critical thinking: Tools for taking charge of your professional and personal life* (3rd ed.). Upper Saddle River, NJ: Pearson Education.
235. Pearson. (2012). *The learning curve: Education and skills for life: Lessons in country performance in education.* London: Author. Retrieved from http://thelearningcurve.pearson.com/reports/the-learning-curve-report-2012
236. Peoples, J., & Bailey, G. (2008). *Humanity: An introduction to cultural anthropology* (8th ed.). Belmont, CA: Wadsworth.
237. Peter, L. J., & Hull, R. (1969). *The peter principle: Why things always go wrong.* New York: William Morrow and Company.

238. Pettigrew, T. F. (1997). Generalized intergroup contact effects on prejudice. *Personality and Social Psychology Bulletin, 23*, 173–185.
239. Pettigrew, T. F. (1998). Intergroup contact theory. *Annual Review of Psychology, 49*, 65–85.
240. Pettigrew, T. F., & Tropp, L. R. (2000). Does intergroup contact reduce prejudice? Recent meta-analytic findings. In S. Oskamp (Ed.), *Reducing prejudice and discrimination* (pp. 93–114). Mahwah, NJ: Lawrence Erlbaum Associates.
241. Piaget, J. (1985). *The equilibration of cognitive structures: The central problem of intellectual development*. Chicago: University of Chicago Press.
242. Pinker, S. (2000). *The language instinct: The new science of language and mind*. New York: Perennial.
243. Postsecondary Education Opportunity. (2001). *Enrollment rates for females 18 to 34 years, 1950–2000*. Number 113 (November). Washington, DC: Center for the Study of Opportunity in Higher Education.
244. Pratto, F., Liu, J. H., Levin, S., Sidanius, J., Shih, M., Bachrach, H., & Hegarty, P. (2000). Social dominance orientation and the legitimization of inequality across cultures. *Journal of Cross-Cultural Psychology, 31*, 369–409.
245. Pryor, J. H., De Angelo, L., Palucki-Blake, B., Hurtado, S., & Tran, S. (2012). *The American freshman: National norms fall 2011*. Los Angeles: Higher Education Research Institute, UCLA.
246. Public Service Enterprise Group (PSEG). (2009). *Diversity*. Retrieved from www.pseg.com/info/environment/sustainability/2009/.../diversity.jsp
247. Ratcliff, J. L. (1997). What is a curriculum and what should it be? In J. G. Gaff, J. L Ratcliff, and Associates, *Handbook of the undergraduate curriculum: A comprehensive guide to purposes, structures, practices, and change* (pp. 5–29). San Francisco: Jossey-Bass.
248. Reid, G. B. R., & Hetherington, R. (2010). *The climate connection: Climate change and modern human evolution*. Cambridge, UK: Cambridge University Press.

249. Riquelme, H. (2002). Can people creative in imagery interpret ambiguous figures faster than people less creative in imagery? *Journal of Creative Behavior, 36*(2), 105–116.

250. Roediger, H. L., Dudai, Y., & Fitzpatrick, S. M. (2007). *Science of memory: concepts.* New York: Oxford University Press.

251. Rose, S., & Hartmann, H. (2004). *Still a man's labor market: The long-term earnings gap.* Washington, DC: The Institute for Women's Policy Research.

252. Rosenberg, M. (2014). *The number of countries in the word.* Retrieved from http://geography.about.com/cs/countries/a/numbercountries.htm

253. Schneider, E. C., Zaslavsky, A. M., & Epstein, A. M. (2002). Racial disparities in the quality of care for enrollees in Medicare managed care. *Journal of the American Medical Association, 287,* 1288–1294.

254. Segall, M. H., Campbell, D. T., & Herskovits, M. J. (1966). *The influence of culture on visual perception.* Indianapolis, IN: Bobbs-Merrill.

255. Seifert, T. A., Goodman, K. M., Lindsay, N., Jorgensen, J. D., Wolniak, G. C., Pascarella, E. T., & Blaich, C. (2008). The effects of liberal arts experiences on liberal arts outcomes. *Research in Higher Education, 49,* 107–125.

256. Senge, P. (1990). *The fifth discipline.* New York: Currency/Doubleday.

257. Shah, A. (2009). *Global issues: Poverty facts and stats.* Retrieved from http://www.globalissues.org/artoc;e/26/poverty-facts-and-stats

258. Shapiro, S. R. (1993). *Human rights violations in the United States: A report on U.S. compliance.* Human Rights Watch, American Civil Liberties Union. New York City.

259. Sherif, M., Harvey, D. J., White, B. J., Hood, W. R., & Sherif, C. W. (1961). *The robbers' cave experiment.* Norman, OK: Institute of Group Relations.

260. Shiraev, E. D., & Levy, D. (2013). *Cross-cultural psychology: Critical thinking and contemporary applications* (5th ed.).Upper Saddle River, NJ: Pearson Education.

261. Shoenberg, R. (2005). *Why do I have to take this course? A student guide to making smart educational choices.* Washington, DC: American Association of Colleges & Universities.

262. Sidanius, J., Levin, S., Liu, H., & Pratto, F. (2000). Social dominance orientation, antiegalitarianism, and the political psychology of gender: An extension and cross-cultural replication. *European Journal of Social Psychology, 30,* 41–67.
263. Slavin, R. E. (1995). *Cooperative learning* (2nd ed.). Boston: Allyn & Bacon.
264. Smith, D. (1997). How diversity influences learning. *Liberal Education, 83*(2), 42–48.
265. Smith, D. G., Guy L., Gerbrick, G. L., Figueroa, M. A., Watkins, G. H., Levitan, T., Moore L. C., Merchant, P. A., Beliak, H. D., & Figueroa, B. (1997). *Diversity works: The emerging picture of how students benefit.* Washington, DC: Association of American Colleges and Universities.
266. Stark, J. S., Lowther, R. J., Bentley, M. P., Ryan, G. G., Martens, M. L., Genthon, P. A., et al. (1990). *Planning introductory college courses: Influences on faculty.* Ann Arbor: National Center for Research to Improve Postsecondary Teaching and Learning, University of Michigan. (ERIC Document Reproduction Services No. 330 277 370)
267. Strage, A. A. (2000). Service-learning: Enhancing student learning outcomes in a college-level course. *Michigan Journal of Community Service Learning, 7,* 5–13.
268. Sullivan, R. E. (1993, March 18). Greatly reduced expectations. *Rolling Stone,* 2–4.
269. Supiano, B. (2014, January 22). How liberal-arts majors fare over the long haul. *The Chronicle of Higher Education.* Retrieved from http://chronicle.com/article/How-Liberal-Arts-Majors-Fare/144133/
270. Terenzini, P. T., & Pascarella, E. T. (2004, July). *How college affects students: A third decade of research.* Plenary address to the Academic Affairs Summer Conference of the American Association of State Colleges and Universities. Albuquerque, New Mexico.
271. The Board of Trustees of the University of Illinois. (2005). *Career preparation.* College of Liberal Arts & Sciences, University of Illinois at Urbana Champaign. Retrieved from http://www.las.uiuc.edu/students/career/businesscareers.html
272. The Conference Board of Canada. (2000). *Employability skills 2000+.* Ottawa: The Conference Board of Canada.

273. The Education Trust. (2008). *Funding gaps 2008*. Washington, DC: Author.
274. The Partnership for 21st Century Skills. (2009). *Framework for 21st century learning*. Retrieved from http://www.21stcenturyskills.org
275. Thompson. A., & Cuseo, J. B. (2014). *Diversity & the college experience* (2nd ed.). Dubuque, IA: Kendall Hunt.
276. Tomasho, R. (2009, April 22.). Study tallies education gap's effect on GDP. *Wall Street Journal*.
277. Torres, V. (2003). Student diversity and academic services: Balancing the needs of all students. In G. L. Kramer & Associates, *Student academic services: An integrated approach* (pp. 333–352). San Francisco: Jossey-Bass.
278. Truman, H. S. (1948). *Higher education for democracy*. New York: Harper & Brothers.
279. Tubbs, N. (2011). Know thyself: Macrocosm and microcosm. *Studies in Philosophy and Education, 30*(1), 53–66.
280. UN New Centre. (2010, January 1). *UN opens biodiversity year with plea to save world's ecosystems*. Retrieved from http://www.un.org/apps/news/story.asp?NewsID=33393&CR=envirionmnet&Cr1
281. U.S. Census Bureau. (2004). *The face of our population*. Retrieved from http://factfinder.census.gov/jsp/saff/SAFFInfo-jsp?_pageId=tp9_race_ethnicity
282. U.S. Census Bureau. (2008a). *An older and more diverse nation by midcentury*. Retrieved from http://www.census.gov/Press-Release/www/releases/archives/population/012496.html
283. U.S. Census Bureau. (2008b). *Bureau of Labor Statistics*. Washington, DC: Author.
284. U.S Census Bureau. (2012). *What is race?* Retrieved from www.census.gov/population/race/
285. U.S. Department of Education. (2002). *Profile of undergraduate students in U.S. postsecondary institutions:* 1999-2000. National Center for Education Statistics, Washington, DC: Government Printing Office.
286. Useem, M. (1989). *Liberal education and the corporation: The hiring and advancement of college graduates*. Edison, NJ: Aldine Transaction.

287. Uzzi, B., & Dunlap, S. (2005). How to build your network. *Harvard Business Review, 83*(12), 53–60.
288. Voices. (2009, Fall). Whither the liberal arts? *Chapman Magazine,* 36.
289. Vygotsky, L. S. (1978). Internalization of higher cognitive functions. In M. Cole, V. John-Steiner, S. Scribner, & E. Souberman (Eds. & Trans.), *Mind in society: The development of higher psychological processes* (pp. 52–57). Cambridge: Harvard University Press.
290. Wabash National Study of Liberal Arts Education. (2007). *Liberal arts outcomes.* Retrieved from http:www.liberalarts.wabash.edu/ study-overview/
291. Walsh, K. (2005). *Suggestions from more experienced classmates.* Retrieved from http://www.uni.edu/walsh/introtips.html
292. Wheelright, J. (2005, March). Human, study thyself. *Discover,* 39–45.
293. White, D. G. (2011). *Yoga, brief history of an idea.* Princeton, NJ: Princeton University Press.
294. Willis, J. (2006). *Research-based strategies to ignite student learning: Insights from a neurologist and classroom teacher.* Alexandria, VA: Association for Supervision and Curriculum Development.
295. Yardi, S., & Boyd, D. (2010). Dynamic debates: An analysis of group polarization over time on twitter. *Bulletin of Science, Technology and Society, 30*(5), 316–27.
296. Zajonc, R. B. (1968). Attitudinal effects of mere exposure. *Journal of Personality and Social Psychology, 9,* Monograph Supplement, No. 2, part 2.
297. Zajonc, R. B. (1970, February). Brainwash: Familiarity breeds comfort. *Psychology Today,* 32–35, 60–62.
298. Zajonc, R. B. (2001). Mere exposure: A gateway to the subliminal. *Current Directions in Psychological Science, 10,* 224–228.
299. Zernike, K. (2009, December 29). Making college 'relevant.' *The New York Times, Education Life.* Retrieved from http://nytimes.com/2010/01/03education/edlife/03careerism-t.html
300. Zinsser, W. (1993). *Writing to learn.* New York: HarperCollins.
301. Zohar, D., & Marshall, I. (2000). *SQ: Connecting with your spiritual intelligence.* New York: Bloomsbury.

www.ingramcontent.com/pod-product-compliance
Lightning Source LLC
Chambersburg PA
CBHW080732300426
44114CB00019B/2567